IT'S YOUR TIME

IT'S YOUR TIME

Clear the clutter, clear your mind

Lead a happy, successful life
by learning to manage your time
and the space around you

Joe Cirillo

The Cirillo Company, LLC

Published by The Cirillo Company, LLC, 2003
Ketchum, Idaho 83340

ISBN 0-9744550-0-8

Printed in the U.S.A.

Edited by Premi Pearson, Inklings Editing Services
Cover design by Andy Hawley, Hawley Graphics

MY STORY

Hi. I'm Joe Cirillo.

Welcome to **IT'S YOUR TIME**, and thanks for joining all of the other folks who have applied this Seven-Step Method to learn how to manage their time and the space around them. Before we start turning pages, moving through your home and workplace, I want to make sure that you're thinking of the process you are about to embark on not as a grueling, hit-the-wall chore, but as a fun experience. When we're done, you'll be a happy camper.

I want to tell you a little about me. No, nothing unusual. I'm just a regular Joe—always worked hard, always had fun. That is key.

I managed my own successful business for 30 years before selling it. The last 28 years were very fulfilling, but the first two were one long, ringing wakeup call. I'd always thought that I was very capable of managing my time, had it all together in the organization department. Wrong. Nope, not me—must have been another Joe. My high stress-meter reading after two years in business got me over that fantasy. Outside, the skies were blue, the clouds were white; but inside, different story.

Little voice said to me one day, "Hey, Joe." I said, "You talkin' to me?" Voice said, "Yep, Joe, we need to talk. You want to come out the other end of this business unshredded, you gotta get a grip."

Getting a grip meant recognizing that I hadn't been a good manager of my time and was not doing a very good job of organizing the space around me. A temporary ego hit, a little drop in confidence. No biggie. I knew Joe, and I knew the best was yet to come.

If I wanted to survive and be successful in the rapid-moving world of imports, product-development and mail order, improvements had to be made. If the business was going to make it big time and achieve my goals, I had to learn how to be more efficient—clear the clutter so I could clear my mind. It seemed daunting at first, but then it turned out to be fun.

And as you know, out of the tree of life, a lot of sweet plums fall. Either they drop on you, or you open your hands and catch them. In this case, one dropped on me—but then I picked it up.

Why, I thought, couldn't the method I'd taught myself also work for other people? My employees, for instance, who were all good, hardworking, fun people. When I announced my plan, though, it sounded a bit grandiose: "Hello, everyone. I am going to teach you all how to manage your time and the space around you here at work, to clear the clutter and clear your mind. And, guess what, you might also want to try this at home." Frowns. Silent boos. But not for long.

I knew that if the business was going to thrive, my people had to be happy and liking their jobs. So I created a constructive, outlined format of my method that was easy to follow, and shared it with the entire organization. Amazingly, they bought into it. Each and every one experienced immediate success with this simple process. It even worked for them at home. Their entire lives became less stressful, happier, and more relaxed.

Thus this book, which is designed to share my method with you. If you follow the Seven Steps in the pages ahead, you will also discover a life full of extra time for yourself, your family, and your friends. My method will have a positive impact on your life, as it has on so many others'—and it will open up more opportunities, motivating you to use your extra time more productively.

I have kept the number of pages small for good reason: I don't want you to spend a lot of time reading another book. The minutes you spend reading *It's Your Time* will reward you in stress-free hours for the rest of your life. So, limber up that page-turning finger and exercise those eye muscles. Let's get it done—blast you into Clear Mindville, U.S.A. And let's have fun!

That's the story~
Joe Cirillo

ACKNOWLEDGMENTS

I would like to thank Premi Pearson for her patience, skill, and wonderful creativity in editing *It's Your Time*. It has been a pleasure for me to work with Premi. Her contribution is the reader's reward.

I would also like to thank Nate Rosenblatt and Andy Hawley for their ideas and creative contributions.

And many thanks to my family and friends, for always being enthusiastic about whatever I might do next.

SEVEN EASY STEPS

ACCEPTING THAT YOU COULD BECOME A BETTER MANAGER OF YOUR TIME AND THE SPACE AROUND YOU.

Admit it: Occasionally you miss a phone call because you can't find the telephone handset. Or someone has ended up driving to your house to see if you were still alive after trying multiple times to leave a message on your overloaded answering machine. Or you were late for a party . . . not your usual twenty-minutes-to-an-hour "fashionable" lateness, but an entire week after the event actually happened.

DETERMINE THE FACTORS THAT HAVE BEEN PREVENTING YOU FROM BECOMING A BETTER MANAGER OF YOUR TIME AND THE SPACE AROUND YOU.

Are you in denial? Have you convinced yourself that living in pandemonium and disarray is just part of your lifestyle, your personality? Or do you tell yourself that all that chaos is just "a phase"? (When was the first time you said that? Two years ago? Ten?) Would you feel like a slacker if you had time to do something "non-productive"?

CLEAR THE CLUTTER: MANAGING YOUR TIME BEGINS WITH ORGANIZING THE SPACE AROUND YOU.

Yes, sure, you know where it is, but you just can't find it. . . . When you have completed this step, you'll actually be able to locate the scissors without rifling through four drawers, dropping the stapler on your foot, and trying to use the utility knife instead. When you open the refrigerator, you'll immediately see your favorite jam sitting there, smiling back at you. You'll be standing tall and feeling proud of the "new you"—you, plus a few new skills.

STEP FOUR – Page 75

LEARN TO MANAGE YOUR TIME IN YOUR OWN ENVIRON-MENT, WITHOUT CHANGING WHO YOU ARE. Sounds classy, doesn't it? You will be so well organized you may even know what to do with those extra two hours you have saved yourself. Your old, disorganized, late self will seem like a distant cousin. Once you've eliminated the need to rush from Point A to Point C (skipping Point B because of the half-hour you spent looking for the car keys), you'll be open to enjoying life. You'll be able to smell the roses and, without the pulse pounding in your ears, you'll be able to hear the birds singing, too!

STEP FIVE – Page 87

ACQUIRING THE TOOLS TO ORGANIZE THE SPACE AROUND YOU. I call these HELPER ITEMS. We all need them, and they work. Essential to your success in managing the space around you, they are easy and painless to buy through the mail-order catalog companies listed here. (Guess what? Shopping through catalogs saves you time. No hours wasted at the mall or driving from store to store.)

STEP SIX – Page 99

ACQUIRING THE TOOLS FOR MANAGING YOUR TIME. List of essential and optional items, and the mail-order companies to buy them from, hassle-free. They're easy to find and simple to use.

STEP SEVEN – Page 101

YOUR DAILY GUIDE, OR TICK SYSTEM. AN OUTLINE DESIGNED TO ASSIST YOU IN MANAGING YOUR TIME AND THE SPACE AROUND YOU FROM DAY TO DAY. Don't worry—I won't be following you around. When you're done, I'm done. This is just to help you keep the spirit and stay the course.

Introduction

I want you to enjoy your life more, as I am enjoying mine. You gotta have fun!

The following pages will provide you with a simple roadmap to making your life happier, less stressful, and more comfortable. You will come to understand the important parallel between managing your time more efficiently and organizing the space around you in a way that allows you to become a successful manager of your life—at work and at home.

In this book you'll find helpful information about the setting and reviewing of certain goals, understanding the most effective hours in your day, the importance of prioritizing a daily task and being proactive, and the power of positive thinking—saying to yourself, "Yes, I can do it!" and "Wow! I really did that!" There is no better feeling than being impressed with what have accomplished, whether it's being accepted at the college of your choice, receiving a promotion at work, getting your golf swing right, or even finding the lost TV remote.

It's Easy and It's Fun

My philosophy is, keep things simple and flowing. Unlike other books, this one cuts to the chase, gets to the point. It does not waste your time. An easy read, it takes you where you want to be—quickly. The intention here is not for you to change who you are, your lifestyle, or your personal style. The intention is for you to learn a few new skills and make them part of who you are. All you have to do is decide you are going to do it and set your goal. You will be off the starting line and to the finish line in **SEVEN EASY STEPS**. At each step along the way, you will be more your own person, more confident in who you really are.

Having more fun comes with being more relaxed. Being more relaxed comes with having enough time to do more of the things you want to do in life. If you can laugh at yourself, you're sure to enjoy reading this book and getting into the process. You'll have the last laugh when you can honestly say, "Yes, I have learned to manage my time and the space around me."

**TIME IS OUR RICHEST RESOURCE.
IT IS WHAT WE DO WITH IT
THAT IS IMPORTANT.**

So, ask yourself: "What have I done with my time today?"

**IF YOU FEEL TIME IS PASSING YOU BY,
TAKE ANOTHER LOOK AT IT
AS IT IS PASSING.**

You will see pockets of opportunity opening.

STEP ONE
of
SEVEN EASY STEPS

Accepting that You Could Become a Better Manager of Your Time and the Space Around You

Time is life's biggest and richest resource, available to all of us daily. It is what we do with it that is important.

I'll bet you've often said to yourself, "There are not enough hours in the day," or "If I only had more time," or "Well, that was a wasted morning."

Research has shown that most people lose up to two productive hours each day. The primary reason, the root cause, is the clutter and chaos in the space around them: disorganized closets, overloaded drawers, bulging refrigerators and pantries, overflowing trash pails, piles of paper, and a messy car trying to function as your office on wheels. If you've ever wandered from room to room looking for a place to eat dinner because there isn't room for a plate *and* a glass on the dining room table, you know what I mean. And if you've ever given up on gracious dining entirely and stood over the kitchen sink to eat, dusting the piled-up dishes with another layer of crumbs, you *really* know what I mean.

Managing your time more effectively is easy once you've organized the space around you and cleared the clutter. With this accomplished, you will have made progress on the path toward rewarding yourself with a precious gift—the two hours you have been losing each day.

Managing your time means organizing your time. Organizing your time runs parallel to organizing the space around you. The tangible items you need must fit into the space where you live and work. A closet, a desk, a drawer, a refrigerator, an empty box—all have a limited amount of space. If you try to cram in more objects than can comfortably fit, you'll end up either using only the things on top or in front, or wasting time pulling things out onto the counter or the floor and

3

(maybe, if you take the time) cramming them back in again.

Your daily task schedule also has limited space, in the form of time. An upcoming day in your life can be viewed in the same way as an empty box into which you must fit certain objects. The number of things the box can contain depends on the size and shape of the objects—and so it is with your daily schedule. The moon belongs to everyone; the best things in life are free—but you won't be able to enjoy what is free if you don't free yourself first.

When you approach a blank piece of paper to outline your schedule for the day, you may find many "things to do" racing to be included on the list. But if you allow all of them onto the page, it will be crammed and overloaded—too many words cluttering the paper, representing too many things to fit into any one day. This is where you remind yourself, "Time is life's biggest and richest resource; it is what I do with it that is important."

It's important to understand the value of the time we can all too easily let slip away—but the answer is not to try to cram in more than will fit! Does this schedule sound familiar? *A long morning run before watering and weeding the plants, before going off to an eight-hour workday (plus commute time), a lunch meeting, a 3 p.m. presentation where you'll need to be fresh and alert, a dental appointment after work, grocery shopping, cooking, an evening tennis game, reading, TV, thinking guiltily about that craft or woodworking project you started in 1998. . . . And what about unscheduled time-consumers, such as searching fruitlessly for the right-size coffee filter? Or reluctantly taking that phone call from an old windbag friend who has won more talk-a-thons than you have won tennis matches?*

If this sounds like a day in your life—or if (tell me it's not so) you *wish* your schedule could be this "relaxed," then you have hit the wall, and have probably bounced off it a few times. You are in task overload.

So, do you acknowledge that you could benefit from learning to better manage your time and the space around you? Good! You've completed Step One.

In the pages ahead, you will learn how to portion out the time in your daily schedule so that it all fits, and the essential things all get done—with time to spare for family, recreation, or a relaxed call to a special friend.

Step Two will help you determine the primary obstacles that have been preventing you from becoming a better manager of your time and the space around you, so you can move ahead. Let's put it in gear, get charged up. Do whatever you have to do to stir up the energy. If it helps to put on running shoes, eat a power bar, or have a cup of java, let's do it and move on. I *know* you can do this!

STEP TWO
of
SEVEN EASY STEPS

Determine the Factors that
Have Been Preventing You from Becoming a Better Manager of
Your Time and the Space Around You
(Until Today!)

Ready to "get real"?

Please ask yourself the following questions—and be as truthful as possible in your answers. Taking a look at your habitual thought patterns will assist you in clearing the way so you can proceed and quickly learn to make the changes you've been wanting to make in your life . . . and it can even be fun!

1. ARE YOU A PROCRASTINATOR?

a. No. It's just that I have to put off a couple of things in order to finish the stuff I didn't get done last week.

b. Well, I function better under stress.

c. I prefer to think of it as being laid-back.

d. Yes, but if I put something off long enough, it sometimes turns out it didn't really need to be done after all—or someone else ends up doing it for me.

e._____ .

2. DO YOU SPEND TOO MUCH TIME ON UNIMPORTANT THINGS AND ISSUES?

a. Well, they seem important at the time.

b. Maybe, but the big things take too much time and energy, and I get overwhelmed easily.

c. It depends on what you mean by unimportant. Computer games are very challenging, and they develop hand-eye coordination.

d. How can I tell my mother that I don't want to hear the two-hour version of her cat's mysterious skin ailment and visits to the vet? She might think I don't care.

e._____ .

3. DO YOU CREATE AN UNREALISTIC SCHEDULE THAT YOU CANNOT ACHIEVE?

a. Well, yes, but if I could just get out of bed when the alarm goes off, I could fit it all in. Six hours of sleep is plenty.
b. My schedule *is* realistic. I just always seem to get behind the slowest tortoise on the road.
c. Maybe if I drank straight shots of espresso instead of lattés, I'd be able to move like a Jetson instead of a Flintstone.
d. What schedule?
e._____ .

4. DO YOU MAKE LONG LISTS OF THINGS TO DO, BUT RARELY IF EVER COMPLETE THEM?

a. Well, I *should* be able to do all of those things. Everyone else does.
b. Maybe, but it doesn't matter because no one else sees the list.
c. I could get everything done if only nothing unexpected would happen.
d. So what? I like making lists. At least I feel like I'm accomplishing something.
e._____ .

5. DO YOU START PROJECTS, BUT NOT COMPLETE THEM?

a. I get bored. It's a sign of intelligence.
b. I *told* my wife she should hire somebody to refinish that deck.
c. Have you ever *tried* hanging wallpaper? Anyway, on all four walls, it might be too much.
d. Who has the time to start a project, much less finish one?
e._____ .

6. ARE YOU CONSISTENTLY LEAVING OUT ITEMS THAT YOU INTENDED TO PUT AWAY?

a. Only if they're nontoxic and not likely to cause spontaneous combustion.
b. If I put the sander and the brushes and the stain back in the garage, my husband will *never* finish that deck.
c. It's easier to have the things I use every day/week/year within reach.
d. This house would not exactly win an award for storage space.
e._____ .

7. ARE YOU FREQUENTLY LATE FOR APPOINTMENTS?

a. Yes, but everyone is used to it.

b. Not really—hardly anything starts when it's supposed to, anyway.

c. Maybe, but it's always for a good reason.

d. I'd be on time if only those self-righteous tortoises didn't insist on driving five miles under the speed limit. It's hard to pass them when it's snowing.

e._____ .

8. DO YOU OFTEN UNDERESTIMATE THE TIME IT TAKES FOR A PROJECT AT WORK OR AT HOME?

a. Things just shouldn't take that long.

b. Not really. It's just that my wife or the dog or my boss or the phone is always interrupting me.

c. Well, that's kind of like always being late, isn't it?

d. If I say how long I really think it's going to take, people will think I'm incompetent.

e._____ .

9. DO YOU SPEND TOO MUCH TIME WITH SOMEONE BECAUSE YOU CANNOT SAY NO?

a. Nnnn . . . Nnnn . . . Well, maybe.

b. I'm just too nice a person to be rude.

c. That idiot just can't take a hint.

d. Well, after all, she did lose her husband just four years ago, and then she had that operation, poor thing. I think she'll stop being so needy real soon.

e._____ .

10. DO YOU SPEND TOO MUCH TIME YAKKING ON THE PHONE?

a. I don't yak. I listen to my sister yak until my ear is sore and my neck has a pinched nerve from gripping the phone hands-free while preparing dinner, eating, and washing the dishes. *She* should read this book.

b. It's only polite to wait for someone to finish telling their longwinded story about their search for replacement parts for that

ridiculous antiquated furnace before you fill them in on the much
more exciting details of your fishing trip in the Rockies.

c. How else would I stay in touch with my loved ones?

d. I have a great calling plan with unlimited evening, weekend, and
wee-small-hour-of-the-morning minutes. If I didn't use them, it
would be like throwing money away.

e._____.

11. DO YOU FIND YOURSELF BUYING ITEMS ON IMPULSE THAT YOU DO NOT NEED?

a. Only when they're on sale. And I'm going to use all that fabric the
minute the kids leave the nest and I can set up a sewing room.

b. Well, I may not need all those batteries/flashlights/key rings/satin
slippers/guidebooks to exotic places right *now*, but if there's ever a
shortage, I'm set.

c. Define "need." The canned goods have to be replaced in the bomb
shelter every year, or they could be dangerous.

d. It doesn't really matter, because when I donate them to the thrift
store, someone who does need them gets them, and I get a
tax deduction.

e._____.

12. ARE YOU ALWAYS GOING OVER YOUR HOUSEHOLD BUDGET BUYING ITEMS YOU ALREADY HAVE, BUT CAN'T FIND?

a. *Don't* tell my husband.

b. If there's ever a shortage, I'm set.

c. What budget?

d. It will all even out in the end—I'm bound to use up or wear out
the originals sooner or later, and I won't have to buy replacements.

e._____.

13. ARE YOU OFTEN LATE PAYING YOUR BILLS?

a. Well, yes, but what difference does it really make?

b. If I could balance my checkbook, I might have more confidence
that I have the funds to cover the bills when they're due.

c. I like the challenge of being charged interest, and then calling the company to complain that their bill arrived late.

d. I would pay them if I could find them.

e._____.

These are typical patterns for many people who have problems organizing themselves and their time. Human beings can be quite creative in coming up with excuses, but if you step back a bit, they all sound pretty much the same. If you answered yes, however grudgingly, to even a few of these questions, recognizing your habitual patterns and being willing to change them will launch you in the right direction.

Did the words "willing to change" make you want to shut the book and take a nap? Stay with me now, and don't get upset. This is not a big deal. Nothing major here.

Change can be good, but you must have the desire to accept it. And it doesn't mean you have to change who you are. On the contrary, it will be up to you to determine what needs to change or be modified in order for you to let go of patterns that are keeping you from living *your* life to the fullest, pursuing *your* goals, feeling at home in *your* own skin. These Seven Steps offer you the opportunity to better manage your time and the space around you through a few simple changes in your environment that will enable you to live, work, and relax in the style that is *you*.

Having the space around you organized does not mean everything has to be neat and tidy. There are many organized people who manage their work time well without having an immaculate desk; they do know, however, what is on and in the desk, and where to find it— without shuffling through piles of odds and ends with an increasing sense of panic and urge to curse. And, most likely, there are no ancient Rolodex cards, apple cores, or year-old "to-do" lists in the mix.

If you recognized some of your patterns in the above-listed questions and answers, and if you are willing to learn how to change them, then you are ready to move on to Step Three. You've made a good start.

STEP THREE
of
SEVEN EASY STEPS

Clear the Clutter:
Managing Your Time Begins with Organizing
the Space Around You

Before we move on, I'd like to share a story about my neighbor Sarah. Sarah was reliably consistent about certain things, but unfortunately not in ways that were beneficial. She could absolutely be counted on, for instance, *not* to put things back in place after using them. I had learned the hard way not to loan her my snow shovel (buried under the eaves until spring), umbrella (left in a taxi), or jumper cables (returned eventually, but only after her new puppy had found them on the garage floor and gnawed through the plastic).

Although I appreciated the energy she expended in finding a replacement umbrella for me (*just* like the original, except that it didn't open and close with the push of a button, and had a border of happy rainbows), I suggested to her that she might like to hear about my method for organizing her space and managing her time. She shook her head, backing away with a look on her face that would have indicated to a casual passerby that I had made a proposition of a much more personal—and unsavory—nature.

The following Christmas Eve, Sarah invited our family and a few other friends and neighbors over for a buffet dinner. When we arrived, Sarah was near tears. She could not find her expensive heirloom silverware, which, she was absolutely certain, had been stolen from the middle drawer of the dining room buffet where it was kept—amongst other things. She had looked high and low, in all the places she habitually stashed things when she was in too much of a hurry to put them away.

For the buffet dinner, Sarah took an assortment of everyday flatware out of the dishwasher and set it next to the plates on the only clear wedge of counter remaining in the kitchen. (The buffet was laden with the shopping bags, magazines, modeling clay, unopened mail, ski hats, goggles and gloves that, until a few hours before, had been occupying the dining table). Her voice shaking, she reported the theft of the silverware to the police department and the insurance company.

Two weeks later, Sarah rang my doorbell, embarrassed but resolute. She had found the set of silver in the trunk of her car, where it had been riding around since April, when she had taken it with her to her sister's house for Easter brunch.

Guess what? Sarah read *It's Your Time*, and she can now find the silverware. As well as the snow shovel, the umbrella, and the jumper cables.

CLEARING THE CLUTTER

Managing your time begins with organizing the spaces where you live and work. We'll be covering a lot of ground to get this accomplished, but we'll be doing it together, one small area at a time. And when we're finished, you'll be amazed at how easy it was to give yourself a sense of calm, a clear mind, and two hours a day to spend any way you wish! Believe it or not, it is this simple.

A cluttered closet and a cluttered schedule are one and the same. Both must be organized to attain the most efficiency, so that time is saved, not lost or wasted.

Clearing the Clutter Clears Your Mind . . .

. . . and a clear mind can easily accept the daily task of managing time effectively. Clarity allows the conscious side of your mind to interact with the subconscious. If you keep a clear mind, you will soon discover that your subconscious is becoming a cheerleader instead of a naysayer.

I am sure you can recall times when you were consciously concerned about getting something done or making an important decision, and "some part" of you just couldn't get with the program. Maybe it even seemed to sabotage your plans. That "part" was probably a subconscious litany of all the old reasons *not* to believe you could get it done.

If you have a clear mind, the subconscious is always in the background saying, "Yes, you can!" (And if an old, negative thought comes up, you'll be able to notice it for what it is—just an old tape—and you can laugh at it and send it on its way.) Several common clichés have their roots in the recognition of this truth: "Mind over matter." "The power of positive thinking." "Accentuate the positive and eliminate the negative." These reminders can be helpful to you in moving ahead and managing your time, but first we must organize the space around you.

HELPER ITEMS

Recommended Helper Items will be listed before each space or area we will be reorganizing. Before you begin the process in each room, make sure you have gathered as many of these items as possible. They will contribute to keeping you organized and saving you those extra two hours in each day. You may already have some of these things sitting in a drawer, at the bottom of a closet, or in your basement. You may also be able to fashion some of them out of materials you have on hand. If not, no problem! Simply turn to Step Five for a list of mail-order companies that will ship these items directly to you.

THE BEDROOM

The Helper Items needed for organizing your bedroom can be found in the mail-order source section in Step Five, page 88.

1. **Dresser drawer dividers**—for separating socks, underclothes, lingerie, pantyhose.
2. **Her jewelry box**—with compartments, for everyday jewelry.
3. **His watch/money valet**—has sections for coins, money clip, wallet, loose credit cards.

The simplest way for you to begin to organize the space around you in a way that fits into your lifestyle is to begin where your day starts—the bedroom. The first thing to do is to put this space in the proper perspective. Most people spend little waking time in their bedroom, but the time they do spend there should be restful, quality time. This space is meant to help you recover, whether it's from an illness or from a busy day. In addition to being the place where you sleep, where you regain your strength in preparation for the next day of activity, the bedroom is your romantic-fun space, and possibly your private "thinking" space. Your day starts and ends here.

Clearing the clutter clears the mind. You want your bedroom to be free of clutter so that when you enter this space to retire, your mind will be clear and your chances will be better for a more restful night's sleep. Certainly, other issues may prevent sleep, but I can assure that you if you keep your bedroom organized and free of clutter, you will feel more relaxed in the evening and in the morning.

❖ Always PUT IT BACK Where It Belongs ❖

We are going to be tackling a lot of reorganization in your home. To make you successful at managing the space around you, everything will be given a place—and it will be essential that you remember to put everything back in place each time you use it.

When you awake in the morning, you want a clear passage to the bathroom. You don't want to see clutter or trip over shoes first thing in the morning. You want a clear mind. As soon as you get up, make the bed. If there are two of you but you don't arise at the same time, have an agreement that the last one up makes the bed. Having a neatly made bed suggests completion to the mind. Night is over, sleep is finished, and the day has begun.

End Tables

Now, stand at the foot of your bed and do a quick evaluation of your end tables. If they are overloaded with magazines, newspapers and books, then we begin here.

Perhaps you've read most of the newspapers and magazines, but they're still here because you don't have a system that reminds you to remove them and stash them in a recycling bin. Or perhaps you think you may want to get back to an unfinished article. In reality, though, if you didn't return to it right away, it probably wasn't important to you—and those magazines may lie there for days or weeks without being opened again.

Take a breath. This is where you bite the bullet, make a rule with yourself: If you have not finished a newspaper within a day or a magazine within a week, it goes out. Day-old newspapers are old news. They belong in the recycling bin. (You may even consider relegating the news to the morning and early evening, banning newspapers from the bedroom completely, since a fresh dose of world events may not be all that conducive to restful sleep.) Keep favorite reading materials in a holding area—a basket or an attractive, sturdy box. Save them for a rainy day or a lazy Saturday morning. On your end tables, keep only a book for a good read, a few current magazines (and possibly the daily newspaper) for a short read, a telephone, an alarm clock, one or two framed photos, and a pen and notepad.

The Dresser

If the top of your dresser holds framed photos, money, notes, jewelry, magazines, books, or papers from work, these items will have to go to their places. You know what to do with the magazines and books. The framed photos are great, but we often allow them to collect in a haphazard way that undermines the special experience of looking at treasured photos individually. Can you thin out the clutter by placing some photos elsewhere? Can some photos be removed from the frames and placed in an album? The money and jewelry will find neat, attractive homes in the containers listed in the Helper Items section.

Now, let's get those dresser drawers organized. This will be easy: Full speed ahead. Have an empty cardboard box or large plastic trash bag nearby to hold items that will be donated to your favorite thrift shop.

Empty all contents onto the bed, separating the items you use often from "inactive" items that rarely or never see the light. It's time to decide what goes to the thrift store. A simple rule to follow: If you haven't worn it or used it in six to twelve months, it's *gone*.

After vacuuming the inside of each drawer, drop the dividers from Helper Items into the top one or two drawers. Roll up all socks, underclothes, lingerie and pantyhose, and place them in the dividers.

Organize your jewelry in its new home, placing each item so that you can see it and make your selection easily. Place the appropriate items in the watch/money valet, arranging them so that each item is visible. Remember those mornings when you couldn't quite get it together, sometimes leaving behind change or bills, or even your credit cards? No more! That's over.

Fold the remaining clothes—jeans, casual shirts, polo shirts, tee shirts, casual blouses, shorts, sweaters, bathing suits—and place them in the drawers of your choice, with the things you wear least often at the bottom. (But remember what to do if "least often" actually means "never.")

You're done! Easy, wasn't it?

THE BATHROOM

First thing after you wake up in the morning, you make a beeline for the bathroom. So that's where we're headed next, bringing along the following Helper Items from Step Five, Page 88):

1. **Cabinet for the toilet area,** available in a wall-mounted or standing floor unit. Provides easy-access storage for toilet paper, facial tissues, paper towels, small hand towels, and washcloths.
2. **Shallow drawer dividers for the top drawers.** Perfect for the things you use once or more each day: toothpaste, toothbrush, dental floss, razor and razor blades, tweezers, nail clippers, nail file, scissors, makeup, hair brush and comb, hair clips and bands.
3. **Compartmentalized dividers that drop into deep drawers,** giving quick access to shaving cream, large medication containers, sunblock, cotton balls and swabs, nail polish and remover, cologne, hairspray and gel. The dividers will keep containers from falling onto their sides and rolling around.
4. **Under-cabinet slide-out organizer** to provide easy, no-mess access to under-sink cleaning solutions.
5. **Under-cabinet slide-out trash pail,** available in several sizes. If (and only if) space is not available under the sink, you'll need an attractive trash container to set on the floor near the sink.
6. **Toilet bowl brush** in an attractive and sturdy, self-contained unit to be kept next to the toilet for easy access.
7. **Soap dish or liquid soap pump.**
8. **Toothbrush holder**—if (and only if) you prefer a unit that stands on the counter. Keep in mind, though, that whatever you leave on the counter will take up space and add to a sense of clutter.
9. **Towel holders**—a variety of options are available. Towel rings, standing hand towel holders, wall-mounted towel racks.
10. **Towel and robe hooks**—attach to the wall by the shower/tub.
11. **Tissue box dispenser.**

The bathroom can be one of the most difficult spaces to keep orderly—and size doesn't matter as much as you might think. We have a tendency to fill up empty space, so a large room can seem just as cluttered as a small one. Whatever the size of your bathroom, though, I can assure you that my method will fit it.

I call the bathroom "the coexist room" because, unless you're lucky enough to have a bathroom for each person in the house, this is the space that is likely to be shared most intimately. (Even the bed has a territory—my side and yours. Once the territory is agreed on, you own it, end table and all.) If your bathroom counters, shelves, and drawers are cluttered and you have trouble finding what you need in the rapid pace of morning, put the Helper Items to work for you.

You should have a towel rack for each person sharing the bathroom. Each rack should contain a bath towel, face towel, and washcloth. A hand-towel ring would be ideal attached to the wall at the end of your sink, or each wall if you have two sinks. If wall space is not available, a standing towel rack would work; it may also be possible to mount a ring on the side of the sink cabinet. If your towel racks are not within reach of your shower/tub, a towel hook should be attached to the wall nearby, providing quick access and avoiding drips across the floor.

But what about all the small stuff that causes clutter and mess? Little items from tubes of lipstick to cans of hairspray seem to appear on surface areas and stay there. These items may be small, but there tend to be a lot of them, jostling each other for space and creating a confusing hodgepodge. As with an overgrown cluster of photographs, after a while, you can't see what you're looking at. The surface next to the sink is likely to be covered with makeup, face creams, shaving creams, razors and razor blades, hair brushes and blow-dryer, nail polish and remover, toothpaste, toothbrushes, deodorant, facial tissue, and cotton balls. It may even be the holding area for replacement bottles of shampoo and conditioner, waiting for their slot on the tub ledge. (Which, by the way, should hold only items that are used on a daily basis. The patchouli oil your cousin gave you three Christmases ago, the expensive facial mask that turned out not to do much except irritate your skin, the collection of tiny bottles from the hotel where you stayed last August, the slightly musty loofah, the rubber ducky your brother gave you as a joke . . . all of it needs to be swept off the ledge and into the trash bag.)

The cabinet below the sink is likely to be a jumble of old sponges, cleaning solutions, back scrubbers, rolls of toilet paper, and the toilet bowl brush—not a place you gladly reach into on cleaning day. Lower drawers tend to be loaded with seldom-used personal-care appliances and old towels (or perhaps, if you tend to save things, brand-new towels that are "too nice" to use). The medicine cabinet and top shallow drawers are almost inevitably loaded with what you may need, and overloaded with what you don't need—outdated medications, stretched-out Ace bandages, partially used ointments, old toothbrushes, rusty nail clippers, tweezers and scissors that don't work effectively.

If you are guilty of harboring all or part of the above, then where better than the bathroom to come clean? Get ready to jump into action, and bring along a heavy-duty trash bag.

Be strong, now. This is your opportunity to do what you always wanted to do, but kept putting it off. Procrastination is *over*. Changes are about to happen—and you'll see that it can actually be fun to let go of what you don't need. You may have begun to throw some of this stuff out before, but avoided it by thinking, "I might need this in the future." That's a trap. The reality is, if you haven't used it in weeks or months, you don't need it. Keep only what you are actually using daily, weekly, monthly, or (as with plastic bandages) when needed. Get rid of all crumbling sponges and old bottles with a bit of gooey liquid left at the bottom.

The cabinet under the sink should contain only cleaning items and solutions, including glass cleaner. Keeping a clean mirror helps keep a clear mind. This cabinet should also contain a trash pail, but never let it get overloaded. It may be out of sight, but if it's too full, it becomes clutter—and it will register that way in your conscious or subconscious mind every time you open the cabinet door to drop trash in. Can't let that happen. Slide-out trash pails can be found in the Helper Items section, as well as a slide-out organizer to keep your cleaning items from becoming an inaccessible jumble. If your cabinet isn't large enough to hold a trash pail, invest in an attractive model for the floor.

The type with a lid and a "step-on" lever will keep the trash out of sight.

The name of the medicine cabinet says it all. Medications and first-aid supplies belong in here, plus toothpaste, floss, and other dental care items if you prefer to keep them in this location. (Remember—if it's outdated or worn out, it's *gone*.)

If you have an inexpensive toilet bowl brush, trash it. Anything so ugly and flimsy will end up rattling around under the sink, if it isn't there already. You need quality and good looks here. The notion of an attractive toilet bowl brush may seem over-the-top, but think about it: If you have to look at something every day, it should look good. And you want it accessible, right next to the toilet, in its own holder.

If you're not happy with your current soap dish or toothbrush holder, facial tissue dispenser or bathmat, go for the gusto. Replace them with versions that are at least as attractive as your new trash pail and toilet bowl brush! If your towel racks and towel rings aren't adequate, go ahead and do it right.

Now, let's finish getting this bathroom together. Drop the drawer dividers into the top, shallow drawer or drawers. It's your call as to what goes in each compartment, but my recommendation is: makeup and creams, razor and razor blades, hairbrush and comb, nail polish and remover, toothpaste and brush, deodorant, nail clippers, tweezers, scissors, and ointments. If you don't have a medicine cabinet, medications and small first-aid supplies should also go here. Drop the larger compartments into the deeper drawers, and use them to store extra shampoo and conditioner, hairspray and gel, sunblock, cologne, cotton balls and swabs, hand soap, and appliances. Any remaining cabinets can be used for extra bath towels. With the clutter cleared and all of your stuff in its own place, it will be so easy to . . . Put It Back!

THE CLOSET

Helper Items recommended for the closet can be found in the mail-order source section, Step Five, Page 89.

1. **Cedar wardrobe closet** on wheels, with a canvas shell, steel frame, and cedar floor. Stores seasonal clothing. Alternatively, a jumbo **vinyl zippered storage bag** can be used. **Under-bed drawers** are

also available for extra drawer space and seasonal clothes.

2. **Shelf dividers** that mount on a closet shelf are ideal for folded sweaters, casual shirts, sweats.

3. **Plastic hangers** to replace those old, wire freebies. Your clothes will hang better and be less likely to develop odd juts at the shoulders—and you'll never again try to remove one hanger from the rod only to end up engaged in battle with a tangled, modern-art mobile of bristling wire. (Your dry cleaner will recycle the old hangers for you.)

4. **Tie/belt/accessory holder**—wall-mounted or hanging.

5. **Multiple pants hanger**—mounts on the wall, and holds either 10 or 20 pairs of pants vertically.

6. **Spring-adjustable hanging rod**—installs instantly without tools or hardware.

7. **Hat rack**—wall-mounted unit for hats, hanging unit for caps.

8. **Shoe storage**—36-pair unit hangs on the inside of a hinged door. Vinyl hanging unit holds purses and bags, or 10 pairs of shoes. Alternative **under-bed shoe and bag storage** slides out easily.

9. **Heavy-gauge Brinks safe**—protects valuable jewelry, extra cash, travelers' checks, credit cards, passports, and important documents. Installs easily on a closet shelf or in a dresser drawer.

10. **Mini stepladder**—folds compactly. Perfect for high closet shelves.

For most of us, our clothes closet is one of the most personal spaces in our home. Our clothing reflects and projects our self-image, and can almost seem to become part of who we are.

In Step One, I referred to the spaces in your daily life into which you must fit the objects you own. In even the most spacious home, the capacity for storage is limited, and the collection of items requiring a place to reside must be limited correspondingly to avoid confusion.

Overstuffed closets are the unfortunate rule in most households. The common excuse, "My closet is too small for my/our clothes," could be a real issue in a tiny house or in a one-bedroom apartment, but the reality is that most Americans have more clothes than they need. I call these inactive clothes. Even if you are not a "clothes horse" and actually have a small selection, you're still almost certain to have inactive pieces. We just enjoy wearing some clothes more than others, the same way we tend to play a few favorite CDs over and over again. The favorites always get time on the street; they're always going out. But what about the "unfavorites"? They have their reasons for not being popular, yet being allowed to lurk in the closet: You don't like the color or the look but don't want to admit they were a waste of money; the style is out but you think it may come back; they don't quite fit, but you're still hoping you might lose those extra pounds.

Then there are the new additions to your large, extended family of clothing. You were out shopping, saw something that was too good a deal to pass up. But did you happen to ask yourself those rather relevant questions, "Do I need it?" and "Do I already have one?" Well, even if you did, you probably weren't sure of the answer. How could you know what you need or already have in that overstuffed closet?

What we are about to do may be simple, but it represents a break-through. It will get you past one of the things that's been preventing you from seeing the light—your jam-packed closet. It's time to stop procrastinating and let go of those inactive clothes and accessories. Remember the feeling of release and accomplishment when you cleared out those old bathroom items? That was just a foretaste of the sense of well-being that will be yours when you get rid of the clutter in your closet.

Bringing several large, heavy-duty plastic bags with you, open the closet door and plunge in. Begin removing EVERYTHING, one piece at a time, and determine whether it is active, inactive (and destined for donation to a thrift store), or trash (even at thrift store prices, no one really wants a shirt with a grease stain on it). Place each article in one of three designated areas in your spacious, uncluttered bedroom: active articles on the bed, separated according to seasonal use; inactive thrift-store donations temporarily stashed on the floor or on a chair (but not between the closet and the bed). You know where to put the trash.

When deciding which articles of clothing are inactive, there is an easy rule to follow: If you haven't worn it in six to twelve months, let it go. Get over it. And if the notion of a garage sale crosses your mind, banish the thought. (Clothing sells for next to nothing at yard sales, and you'd be wasting space storing the stuff and wasting time trying to bargain with the guy who wants to pay 50 cents, not a dollar, for that slightly itchy merino sweater.) You may come across some "iffy" actives—clothes you've worn at some point during the last twelve months, but didn't quite enjoy wearing. If you're not sure, try the item on in front of a full-length mirror. If it isn't comfortable, you'll know without even looking; but if it is comfortable, check it out in the mirror. Does it hang right? Do you feel at ease and attractive in it (or at least "as attractive as it gets")? If not, it's gone. And first impressions are accurate—no second-guessing.

The journey through your clothing maze is almost guaranteed to turn up some discoveries: "Wow, look what I found! I forgot I had this!" Or, "I've been looking for this for months"—good news, unless you just bought another one last week. When (not yet!) you replace the active "keepers" in the closet, you'll probably feel a new sense of appreciation for the clothes that made the cut. You'll be able to see and enjoy them. What-to-wear decisions will be a snap—no more dithering or meltdowns. And when you are out shopping, there will be less pressure and confusion, since you will know what you have and what you need.

In the removal process, don't forget to apply the rule to coats, jackets, handbags, shoulder bags, belts, ties, shoes, and boots. Whether they were the bargains of the century or buyer's-remorse splurges, whether they are beautiful and stylish or clunky and outmoded . . . if they no longer fit or have become a member of the inactive club for any other reason, they're out. (If it's a few years old but still looks brand new, that is NOT a reason to hold onto it—just the opposite, as a matter of fact.) Do not waver when it comes to those piled-up shoes. If they haven't been stepping out, hitting the pavement in six to twelve months, they are inactive. (And, no, it won't count if you cram your feet into those elegant but excruciating five-inch heels right now and totter out to the mailbox. This calendar counts backward, not forward, and promising yourself that you'll change your lifestyle to fit your shoes is counterproductive in more ways than one.)

If you have any luggage stored in your closet—or boxes of souvenirs and memorabilia, extra bed linens, skeletons—remove them, as well. Now take a look at your empty closet. Wow, bigger than you thought! It even has walls! And you're about to take advantage of it while it is bare: Bring in the vacuum cleaner. It's been a while.

Next, fold all of the inactives and place them in the plastic bags designated for the thrift store. No need to bother folding the trash. If you've dodged the decision on a couple of things and left them placed ambiguously in between the active and inactive areas, you're only human . . . but, since you're reading this book, you're a human who's decided to make a fresh start and stop wasting time. If you're not sure at this point whether something is a keeper, it's not. So, without further hesitation, put those things into the plastic bags, where they belong. Ahh.

Now it's time to face your collection of wire hangers. If you don't get rid of them, they'll just hang around. Keep only what you need and, preferably, replace all wire versions with large, sturdy plastic or wood hangers. Your clothes will like them better, and so will you.

Okay, now we're ready to put those Helper Items to good use. This isn't going to be difficult, and it won't take long, so don't resist. Think positive and remind yourself, "Two hours a day." That's right—closet efficiency contributes to getting those hours back.

Depending on the storage unit you have selected, fold or hang all seasonal clothing for the season that has just past. With the inactives gone and the seasonals in hibernation, you'll have a good burst of energy. You're about to get it right!

If the ceiling is high enough and you have more than one wall that will accommodate hangers, install spring rods to give yourself at least two tiers for hanging shorter items such as shirts and blouses. Position the dividers on the closet shelf or shelves in whatever order will work best for you. Hang the metal shoe rack on the door or the vinyl rack on a rod (or both). It's best to hang the vinyl unit near a wall. If you have selected the under-bed shoe unit or the under-bed drawers, set them near the bed. Install the pant-hanging and tie/belt/accessory units. If you have selected wall models, the most accessible wall is ideal. Install the hat rack, preferably at the highest reachable point in the closet. Place the optional cap-hanging unit in an out-of-the-way location unless you wear caps every day.

Now you are ready to Put It Back.

Hang all pants, and then hang all ties, belts, and other accessories.

Place folded sweaters, casual shirts, and sweats in the shelf dividers. Put your shoes in pairs in their storage unit, along with handbags and shoulder bags. Hang any hats and caps. If you don't have a hat rack, utilize any extra shelf space. Purses can also find a place on shelves. Hang shirts, blouses, additional pants, suits, dresses, and sports jackets in the order that best works for you, with the items you wear often most easily accessible.

You'll probably find yourself with plenty of room for outer garments that have been crowding your front-entry closet or the hooks on the wall by your back door. (Remember, though, before ANYTHING ever goes into your closet again, it must pass the "active" test.) If you do not have space elsewhere for your luggage, you probably have floor space in the closet now to hold it comfortably. Boxes of memorabilia should be moved to the attic or the basement, and skeletons can take a hike.

So, are you impressed with what you have accomplished? Sure you are! And now that you have breezed through these areas, you can easily apply the same method to additional bathrooms and closets.

If you want to experience the freedom of being organized and save those two hours a day, you'll have to follow up on yourself. Put It Back instead of leaving it out in whatever location seems convenient at the time. Be consistent, and your stuff will always be in place, ready whenever you are. With no clutter in the way, it will be simple. You can do it.

One more thing—a win-win situation. Don't let those bags of inactives sit around in your mudroom or basement. Take them, today, to your local Goodwill, Salvation Army, or any other organization that makes clothing available to people in need. You'll get a tax benefit, and someone else will enjoy the clothing you no longer enjoy. Get those "inactives" out on the street again.

THE KITCHEN, REFRIGERATOR, and PANTRY

Recommended Helper Items can be found in the mail-order source section, Step Five, page 90.

1. **Trash pullout slider**—installs under the sink, keeping messy trash out of sight and eliminating odors while remaining accessible for instant trash removal. If there is not enough room under the sink

or you prefer not to install the hardware, use an attractive covered trash container, either with a step-on lever that raises and lowers the hinged lid, or with a push flap that shuts after trash is inserted.

2. **Under-sink slide-out shelf**—installs under the sink. Ideal for keeping cleaning solutions neat, organized, and accessible. Alternatively, use a divided plastic "toolbox" with a handle.

3. **Spice drawer organizer**—drops into a drawer near your stove. If you don't have the drawer space, a rotating spice organizer can be placed either on the counter or in a cabinet.

4. **Condiment rack or turntable**—can be stored in a drawer or "appliance garage," or on the counter.

5. **Knife organizer**—for carving knives or a combination of carving and steak knives. Use a block type on the counter for easy access, or drop a drawer-type organizer into a drawer in the prep area.

6. **Junk-drawer organizer**—a must for every home.

7. **Refrigerator can holder**—eliminates can clutter in the fridge.

8. **Butter dish/egg holder**—assists in keeping the fridge organized.

9. **Hanging pantry organizer**—hangs inside the pantry door. If you have a cabinet-style pantry, use turntable, **pullout and multi-shelf units** for quick, easy access at a glance.

10. **Folding 9-inch stool**—for reaching the top shelf.

11. **Pullout pot lid organizer**—installs in a cabinet near the stove. Keeps the right lid handy and within reach of the right pot.

12. **Pot rack**—If ceiling space is available over the stove, this is the ideal location for a variety of cookware. Easily accessible, decorative, and frees up cabinet space.

13. **Cabinet dividers**—for platters, cookie sheets, baking dishes. Vertical dividers eliminate clattering "landslides."

14. **Cookbook caddy**—can be stored in a cabinet. Easy-grip handle.

15. **Key rack, outgoing mail shelf**—No more lost keys, no more wondering if the mail made it to the post office.

You know what they say: "If you can't stand the heat, get out of the kitchen."

Well, this is your moment of truth. Some people love to be in the kitchen, and some hate it. Others have a love/hate relationship—love to cook, hate to clean up. To avoid the issue, some people skip break-fast and hit the nearest shop. But, for most of us, dealing with the kitchen is a necessity whether we like it or not, and since it is the first place we visit each day after the bedroom and bathroom, here we are.

Coffee, tea and toast, juice and a multiple vitamin, bacon and eggs . . . whatever your breakfast routine is, the kitchen plays a role in starting almost everyone's day. This is an important space, and it should feel good and smell good.

You might think of the kitchen as the hardest space to get organized and kept that way, but no. We'll soon have it under control.

Let's start with your morning java or tea. If you have a coffeemaker with a timer, evening prep will eliminate some of the morning rush and give you the few minutes it takes to clean the pot—and I don't mean a casual rinse. Unwashed coffeepots eventually build up a filmy residue that deprives you of the wonderful aroma and fresh flavor that make coffee a joyful way to start the day. So keep it clean, and you'll keep coming back for more. Making your own coffee or tea saves money and time, and gives you several peaceful, quiet moments to listen to a favorite piece of music or read an inspiring thought for the day.

Kitchens of all sizes have been designed to be functional, but they can easily become dysfunctional, especially if space is at a premium. If yours is anything like Doug and Judy's, you are in big trouble. Theirs was in clutter-overload mode at all times. The counters were groaning under opened and unopened mail, magazines, newspapers, dust-gathering appliances from espresso machines to pasta presses, tools waiting to return to abandoned home-improvement projects, kitschy ceramic wedding presents, and an economy-size bundle of paper towel rolls with nowhere else to go. The fridge was loaded with little jars of gour-met condiments too expensive to throw away but too peculiar to eat. The trash pail had a perpetual pile of recyclable bottles and cans leaning into it, eager to crash onto the floor with the least provoca-tion. Doug blamed Judy, and Judy blamed Doug—an excellent exchange of equal denial.

Judy came home one day and said to Doug, "Enough mess is enough. I'm tired of our kitchen looking like Sanford and Son's, and arriving at work to find last week's newspaper in my attaché case." That became their moment of truth.

Then there was Elizabeth Dunkin. She was the Queen of Clutter, but never mind—she loved cooking and baking from scratch. The problem was, she wasted too much of her precious time in the kitchen searching for "missing" implements and ingredients. Her moment of truth came when she was unable to find the TV remote control for two days. When it did show up, it was someplace she never would have thought to look—in the fridge, under a carton of eggs. She had no idea how that had happened, but it served as a turning point.

Your kitchen, like everyone else's, contains more stuff than any other place in the home. So, stand back and do a visual check. Are your counters loaded with bottles of water, wine or soda, bags of bread, condiments, groceries not put away, piles of opened and unopened mail, paid and unpaid bills, newspapers and magazines, keys, checkbook, cookbooks, outdated notes to yourself and family members, dried-up flowers in skuzzy vase water, unwashed dishes, dishes washed but not put away, clean laundry that hasn't yet been Put Back, skittery CDs looking for a home, a telephone handset missing its daily juice-up time? Not to mention the usual toaster, coffeemaker, blender, food processor, and microwave.

Clutter results partly from habit, partly from procrastination, and partly from a feeling of being rushed, with no time to put things away. I understand. The fact is, you haven't had the time. But we're going to fix that. We're going to clear the clutter, clear the way for your mind to take charge of managing your time. No need to worry or feel overwhelmed. There is a beginning to everything, and the best is yet to come.

The Counters

Okay, here we go. Take a deep breath and grab four or five heavy trash bags, depending on whether plastic is recyclable in your area. (If you haven't been consistent about recycling, now is the perfect time to start. In addition to being much better for the environment, recycling will assist in keeping you organized.) Designate one bag for paper, one for glass, one for cans, one for plastic (if applicable), and one for trash. From the counters, dump all old newspapers into the "paper" bag, along with unneeded and junk mail if it's recyclable in your area (if not, it goes into the "trash" bag).

The Refrigerator

From the fridge, remove all glass and plastic containers you no longer use (or have never used), all outdated containers, and anything with a hint of mildew. Dump the remains down the garbage disposal or into a sealed container to be disposed of in the trash, rinse out the containers, and place them in their designated bags. Same process for cans. If you have unopened containers of food that you know you won't use, pick up the phone and call a family member, a friend, or an organization that takes food products. Give it away.

Any vegetable or fruit at any stage of decay has got to go. It's not healthy to keep last week's "fresh" foods around. Declaring them a loss opens the way to using the new, younger produce that's been waiting for you to grimace your way through the old stuff.

Now remove all keeper items, and survey the interior walls and empty shelves of your fridge. It's probably a good time for a visit with Mr. Clean.

Before we replace your refrigerated foods, let's evaluate applicable Helper Items. We want the interior of your fridge to make you feel happy and in control. When you open the door, the fresh, delicious item you're looking for should be looking right back at you. A six-can or twelve-can holder/dispenser and a multi-shelf unit will allow you to stack items neatly. Add a new butter dish and egg holder if you need them, and you are good to go.

On to your overburdened freezer compartment. Freezers just keep taking it all in, no matter what it is—always room for one more, although research has shown that 40 percent of frozen food will develop a severe case of freezer burn and never be eaten. Your freezer is probably overstocked with frozen veggies, potatoes, fruits, desserts, pizzas, TV dinners, chicken, fish, meats, breads, rolls, ice cream products, and so on. For a lot of good reasons, you want backup:

You never know when you are going to have surprise guests, or when a storm will arrive and you won't be able to get to the store. And, of course, you don't want to throw food away. The truth is, though, if you have too much, it is going to go to waste, frozen or not. Use up what you really can, and give the rest away. If it's not going into your stomach, let it satisfy someone else.

Okay, with the freezer done, you've just created another win-win situation. Someone will be having a few good meals as a result of your willingness to share the bounty, and you're more fully in charge of your life. As a bonus, there won't be any more avalanches of rock-hard packages when you open the freezer door.

No, No . . . Not the Pantry!

Yes, the pantry. You can do it. With both of us movin' in, I can assure you that the pantry's army of contents will be movin' out. You will be finished in a very short time, with one more space back in your control.

Take *everything* out of the pantry and put it in one of three places: Group things you're sure you'll use before the expiration date on the countertop. Anything past its expiration date or just plain stale goes in the trash. And usable items you don't need or want should be placed in a box, destined for people who do need and want them. As you're removing items, if you find that you've loaded up on unopened duplicates and triplicates because you had no idea what was in the back reaches of the cabinet, welcome your chance to share the wealth. While you're making that box something the receiver will be overjoyed to unpack, you'll also be giving yourself a way to take stock, at a glance, of all the grocery items you have on hand at any given time.

When the pantry is empty, give it a good vacuuming and wipe down the shelves. Stand back and admire yet another beautiful space, waiting to be beautifully organized.

If your pantry has a regular hinged door, install a hanging door rack that will keep up to 50 food products visible and accessible. If your pantry has cabinet doors, a turntable-style organizer or multi-shelf, pullout organizer (or both) will be very helpful.

Replace the keeper items. If you find that you've created more than enough extra space, use it for everyday placemats and napkins. Now give yourself a pat on the back: you're done. Well, you're done for *the moment*—but you need to plan for the future.

Your pantry, refrigerator, and freezer have become accustomed to making their own rules. Strange things have been happening behind closed doors. You've got to be strong, vigilant in your follow-through: First, Put It Back. Second, add items to a current grocery-shopping list as you use them up or notice that they are almost gone. Third, visit the pantry, fridge, and freezer to take stock before grocery shopping. Now that you can see what you have, you won't buy what you don't need, and you won't spend as much money on food. That's right, less green stuff in the fridge, and more in your pocket.

So, we have created an opportunity—but be forewarned. Along with the opportunity, we have created a potential risk. How? Simple. If you tend to be an impulse shopper, you may quickly fill up that extra room in your pantry, refrigerator, and freezer with "good deals." You know how tempting it can be to go ahead and buy two for the price of one, even if it's a product or a brand no one in your family particularly likes. Before you buy the second bundle of paper towels for 50-percent off, consider whether they're the ones you've come to prefer after years of cleaning up spills, or whether they're the ones you swore you'd never buy again after the last sale suckered you in. A bargain is not a bargain unless you're saving money on an item you would otherwise have bought for full price. And no matter how good the deal may seem, you're paying too much if the cost is your hard-won sense of organization and peace of mind. Limit yourself to one or, at the most, two backup packages of the grocery items you and your family enjoy on a regular basis. Check expiration dates to be sure you will use duplicates while they are fresh, and store them directly behind each other on the shelf, rotating them forward as they are used. If you get in the habit of making regular consultations with your fridge, freezer, and pantry before going grocery shopping, you will stay in control of impulse shopping.

Back to the Counter

Pantry time is over. Let's move along and finish the counter area.

If there are a few condiments you use every day, it's fine to keep them out on the counter as long as they are neat, clean, and organized on a rack or a turntable. An appliance garage is ideal for keeping your toaster, coffeemaker, blender, and food processor close at hand but out of sight. If they must be in view, make sure they are sparkling clean and easy on the eye. If you have a bread-storage container and it works for you, great—but the fridge does at least as good a job of keeping bread fresh. If your microwave sits on the counter and is rather large, you may want to consider getting a smaller unit that will take up less space and operate more efficiently.

And now, back to those paper piles. You've thrown out the old, unwanted mail, but you may still have stacks of paid and unpaid bills with noplace to go. For now, set them aside in two boxes or large envelopes, marked "paid" and "unpaid."

This is a good time to get your keys and outgoing mail organized. You can find the perfect key rack/mail shelf in the Helper Items section. Install it near the door where you exit and enter your home every day. You'll know where to find your keys, and you won't have to wonder whether Aunt Mary's birthday card made it to the post office.

Oh, Those Drawers and Cabinets

Ready to move in and take full command of what lurks behind closed doors (and drawers)? There are good guys and bad guys living in there, and we're going to sort them out—remove the bad guys, tell them their shelf life is over. They can no longer hide.

Let's start with the junk drawer, which probably holds the usual odds and ends—tools, picture hangers, batteries, extension cords, glue, nails, screws, tape, paperclips, scissors, birthday candles, rubber bands, string. It may also be harboring some unusual fugitives, from tie clips and headbands to theater programs and ant traps. You have to wonder, how can so much fit into one drawer? And a lot of it has been in there for a long time, hidden from view by the hammer handle that keeps jamming the drawer. Do you really have any idea of what this drawer has been keeping from you? How many times have you gone looking for the tape but been unable to find it, even if you have been able to yank the drawer open? You've lost time on each occasion, and your solution has probably been to buy a new roll. Wait until we get into that drawer—you'll probably discover three rolls of tape, each clinging to its own assortment of tacks and nameless fuzz.

Helper Items to the rescue! A junk-drawer divider costs very little, and organizing it will give you a chance to get rid of the duplicates. (Yes, you will eventually use all three rolls of tape—but consider placing two of them in other areas in your home where they would come in handy.) If you find loose batteries in the junk drawer, check to be sure they still have a charge, and recycle any that are spent.

Your everyday cutlery probably already has its place in a drawer organizer. If it's adequate and accessible, you don't have to do a thing except lift it out to vacuum and wipe down the drawer. However, if you have broken cutlery or pieces you dislike or never use, they should be removed. Duplicate utility knives and spoons, ladles, spatulas, corkscrews, etc., should also go unless you actually need them. Now that you're familiar with the joys of the letting-go process, it should be easy to pass these space-takers on to someone who could use them.

Your "good" silver or stainless cutlery and serving spoons probably have a place where they are kept between dinner parties; but if not, now is the time to find them a permanent home. (Remember what happened to Sarah.) These items, along with special-occasion serving dishes, placemats and napkins, generally have compartments in a dining-room hutch. If you don't have a hutch, try to create space in a kitchen cabinet or drawer. In a pinch, even a shelf in a linen closet will suffice.

One of the remaining shallow kitchen drawers should contain plastic wrap, baggies, and foil. If you didn't find space in your pantry for everyday placemats and napkins, a shallow or medium-size drawer would be a good home for them. Another medium-size drawer can keep kitchen towels and potholders close at hand. A drawer next to the stove is ideal for your spices. A spice caddy will work if drawer space is limited; place it in a cabinet near the stove for easy access.

Cookie sheets, roasting pans, serving platters, and pizza pans should all be stored near the oven in a cabinet with vertical dividers. (If you need dividers, Helper Items has the fix.)

Pot lids have a way of always being in the way, sliding and clattering around. It's impossible to keep them stacked, and it takes up too much room to keep them partnered with their pot pal. So, what to do? A drawer holding just the lids would solve the problem, but if you're fresh out of drawers, try the pullout lid organizer in the Helper Items section.

Where to keep the pots? The best place is a hanging pot rack. If ceiling space is available over your stove, that's the ticket. Otherwise, a deep, sturdy drawer under the stove works well. A cabinet under a stovetop is less handy, but it will do if it's what you've got.

Along with glasses and cups in many sizes and shapes, from mundane to elegant, you've probably collected everyday dinnerware and place settings for parties and holidays. The time has come to eliminate the duplicates and the damaged. If you've been saving the extras for that second home one day or for a kid's first apartment after college, box them up and find a place to store them. However, if you don't have storage space, extras should go. If and when you need them, new ones are out there, for very little cost.

Once you are down to the real players, separate the things you use daily from those that come out only on special occasions. Your everyday glassware and dinnerware should be like members of your team: when you're cooking, you want them to be within reach, ready and waiting. Pieces that are used less frequently can live in a hutch or a high cabinet. Coffee cups should be kept near the coffeepot, ready to be filled when you're ready to pour.

Before we leave the kitchen, we need to address your collection of cookbooks. Everyone who cooks refers to them, and some of us follow their instructions word for word. But it's likely that you have cookbooks that are functioning only as shelf décor or as representatives of exotic dreams that might have been, but will never be. You may also have a motley collection of tear-out recipes stuffed into an overloaded folder, or piles of magazines you kept for the sake of a few, never-used recipes.

It's good to dream—keep doing that—but trade in your faded dreams for new ones. As elsewhere, sort out what you really need, really use, really like. Be philanthropic with the inactive books, and donate the magazines to the recycling bin. When you've eliminated all but your favorite cookbooks, find space for them in a cabinet near your food-prep area. The cookbook caddy listed in the Helper Items section can be placed in a cabinet, ready to be pulled out when it's time to activate the creative-cooking juices.

One more suggestion before we turn off the lights in the kitchen and move into the dining room: If you have limited space in your kitchen and do not have an eating counter or breakfast nook, you might be able to make great use of a compact, self-contained eating counter/serving area. When folded out, it has four stools; and when folded up, it takes little space. I was impressed with the simple design, efficient use of space, and low cost of this Helper Item.

How are you feeling at this point, o guru of organizing? In no time at all you have whipped together one of the most challenging spaces in the home. You've cooled off the heat. The rest of your home will be a piece of cake.

THE DINING ROOM

No Helper Items are necessary. (Whew!)

The dining room is probably the most sociable area in the home, the place where stories are born, or retold with embellishment after a few glasses of wine. Diners may sit down in a quiet mood, yet finish the meal laughing and loquacious—or, sometimes, in tears. This is the stage for funny entrances and clever repartee. It's also where, if you've risen to the occasion with an impressive new recipe, you might be plagiarized by cunning guests who space their carefully casual ingredient questions throughout the evening. Anyone with a sense of humor has to laugh when the tables are turned and your guests-turned-hosts proudly serve you "their" wonderful new dish. A successful dinner party makes everyone wish the night would never end.

If, on the other hand, the dinners you've hosted simply seemed like they would never end, maybe it's because your home hasn't been set up to be much fun. Tony and Mildred gave many dinner parties when they were first married, looking forward with anticipation to inviting the guests, selecting a fine wine, presenting the food creatively. They repeatedly found themselves disappointed, though, and feeling that the dinner party was too much of a job to be fun. The main result of each occasion was that Tony and Mildred ended up not speaking to each other. Finally, burned out, they threw in the towel. They gave up entertaining and went shopping instead, trying to define who they were as a married couple by the things they bought together instead of by fostering intimacy with a circle of friends. Useless items from each of their shopping sprees found a resting place on the dining room table. Tony and Mildred gradually stopped cooking, consuming take-out food and frozen dinners in front of the TV. If they had a spontaneous urge to cook, they quickly suppressed it, remembering the effort it would take to clear and set the table . . . until they finally got with the program, applied the Seven Steps, invited a few friends over—and had a wonderful time!

The dining room should be the easiest room in the house to keep organized. It has no moving parts, nothing to hang, standard furnishings, and considerable "down time" because most daily meals are eaten in the kitchen. So, what's with the mess, the clutter build-up? It's far too easy, when the dining table is empty and you don't have a designated place for your shopping kill of the day, to unload on the old flat top. Your table has no defenses, and within a few days it can be inadvertently transformed from a serving place to a resting place. And since you have no idea what to do with those items you brought home, your table is carrying the load for you.

So, let's do the usual. Step back and take a look at what, other than shopping bags, is on the table. Let me guess. . . . more piles of paper, right? Bills, blank forms to complete, bank statements, letters to answer, newsletters and magazines to read, insurance policies to review, children's report cards, invitations waiting for a response, medical forms to complete, prescription drugs to fill, and so on. You may have gotten used to these piles, may even think you know what's in each intricate tower, but it's time to say, "So long."

This is a simple fix. First, we'll deal with the boxes and bags of shopping goodies. I'm sure you're not indulging in the impulse-shopping thriller experience anymore, but your dining table may still be bearing the evidence of past excesses. If you still have receipts, return what you don't need. Give anything else that's "extra" to a family member or friend or add it to your boxes of philanthropic contributions. With so much of your home organized now, the useful items should have places to go and things to do.

As we gather our strength to attack the piles of paper, you might want to get yourself reenergized. Do some stretches, have a power bar, drink a cup of tea. Whatever it takes to get ready to clear the deck.

Gently lift the piles off the table and take them to a "temporary holding area" otherwise known as the living room floor. Yes, that's right, the living room floor—an area that is probably clutter-free, but in a room that has not yet been given an organizational going-over. We are asking for its assistance in pile survival.

The dining room is now free again. It may seem a little boring at first, without the excitement all that shopping glamour and guilt, but it's for the best. The room is like a stage waiting for the actors, biding its time until the return of evenings filled with good food, wine, and laughter. Take a little time to buff out the area, and you're done.

THE LIVING ROOM, FAMILY ROOM, DEN

In many homes today, the living area is in the same open space as the dining area. Some homes have a separate family room, which may double as rec room. Your home may have a den, study, office, or a combination.

All of these rooms have aspects of living style in common. It's likely that all or most contain books (including large coffee-table books), magazines, photo albums, framed photos, CDs, a stereo, a TV, and remote controls—items that can form a clutter brigade and turn into the enemy. The best way to fight this enemy and win is to launch a multiple attack on all related rooms at the same time. One space may contain more stuff than another, but use the same methodology in each room.

The Helper Items for these areas can be found in the mail-order source section in Step Five, Page 92.

1. **Magazine racks.**
2. **Remote control caddy.**
3. **Hanging and/or standing bookshelves.**
4. **Photo frames.**
5. **Hanging shelves for framed photos.**
6. **Drawer and/or floor CD organizer.**
7. **Tiered coffee-table book holder.**
8. **End table or ottoman with storage compartments.**

You might feel as if you're about to climb Mt. Everest, taking on more than one space at one time—but not to worry. This is an efficiency move.

First, pile control. Gently lift all remaining stacks of paper and lower them into isolation in the "pile corral" on the living room floor. That will be their designated area until we are ready to render them harmless.

Now, let's move onto magazines and catalogs. (The recycling bin is going to enjoy this.) Gather them all up from all areas, then separate outdated issues of magazines you would like to keep with your books for reference and for educational reasons. Place recent catalogs you know you need and want in a basket or in a magazine rack or box that will hold them vertically. Eliminate all don't-want, do-I-really-need issues.

Magazines have a way of becoming permanent fixtures in your home with their persuasive good looks and promises. We don't need them all and don't usually read them all, but never quite get around to canceling our subscriptions. We like going to the mailbox and finding our "friends" there, waiting to be picked up. When I went through this process of elimination, I cancelled six out of twelve subscriptions to periodicals. I haven't missed them, and the other six have remained good friends.

Now's your chance to do the same. Say you're sorry, but it's over:

pick up the phone or go online and cancel. This move represents a giant step toward reducing clutter in your daily mail and in your home. If you find that you miss one or more of your old friends, you can always revisit them at the nearest store that carries them. Magazine shopping can be fun, like browsing in a bookstore. But be careful. Don't fall into the trap of filling out that self-mailer subscription form. Enjoy the moment.

Now, for those coffee-table books—fun to have, and fun for guests who like perusing them. If your rooms have tabletops spacious enough to hold these books and your coffee too, great—if not, the Helper Items section has a tiered rack that stands on the floor and not only gives you tabletop freedom, but gives the books a new lease on life by bringing them into better view.

Framed photos are a favorite for all of us. We like to look at family members or friends and reflect on the time a photo was taken. Frames can gang up on you, though. Another one is always joining the collection, and as more photos join in, the collection becomes a blur. It gets difficult to see and appreciate each individual photo. What to do? The war on clutter can be emotional at times, and this is one of those times—but there's a Helper Item to get you out of this bind. A hanging shelf is a cinch to install, and will release your framed photos from the clutches of the cluster squeeze. They'll be out on their own, free to express themselves.

Music, music, music. Whatever the new song is, or the new artist, we have to have it. We have been happy consumers of musical reproductions throughout their evolution, from the old, heavy 78 records and vinyl LPs (long-playing records, for those of you too young to remember), single 45s, 8-track cassettes, small cassettes, and digital CDs. Along with this chronological process, we have purchased the corresponding electronic players. It's been fun, but unless you've been consistent about passing along the old while welcoming the new, these constant innovations may have become aging, dust-gathering members of your clutter family.

We are in the here and now. The CD format has been with us for some time, and it looks like it will be here a while longer. Technology is reducing the size and increasing the capacity, but the basic concept is a winner. Some homes might have one stereo system; others might have CD players in all three living areas and in the bedrooms as well. If you're feeling crowded with all of that equipment, it's possible to consolidate by creating one central headquarters and using small speakers in the various rooms. If a central stereo system does not work for you, the mini's will. But—go after those CDs. Select the storage system that's right for you, and bring them in. Before you start Putting Them Back, though, make sure that your CD collection doesn't contain duplicates or mistakes (I'll bet it does). Mistakes are those you've played only once, or gritted your teeth through for a second time, trying to develop a taste for the music. Donate them to your library, where another patron may be absolutely thrilled to be transported by the very sounds that set your teeth on edge. If you get good control of your CD collection, you'll know what you have, and where to find it.

Your television has a working relationship with the cable box or satellite controls, VCR, and DVD player. They all get along well, and they don't tend to roam about the house, looking for other companions. Unfortunately, though, their offspring—those remote controls—are less well behaved. As they increase in numbers and shift positions, traveling from person to person and from room to room, it's easy to end up confused about which remote does what. It may seem there are too many to manage. Remember the lost remote that turned up in the fridge? We don't want that kind of thing to happen. Helper Items to the rescue! A remote caddy will give you a place for everything. All you have to do is remember to Put It Back.

Ah, books. Saved the best for last. As with your CD collection, your library is a case of "gotta have it." Favorite authors keep producing favorite books, and new writers are always in the wings, ready to become new favorites. Trying to get rid of books can be emotionally taxing. You have a relationship with the experience you had while reading them; you've gotten to know the characters intimately. They've become part of your life. You keep books so that you can refer to them, revisit them in a reflective way, and possibly share them with someone else. You want other people to have the same experience you had. Full bookshelves seem, in themselves, a personal statement of accomplishment. If you're a real book hound, volumes may be spread throughout your home. They may even be taking up floor space. If so, you are overbooked!

Try stepping back and taking stock of all the books you own. Better yet, count them. You may be startled by the number. The truth is, it's time for some of those pages to be turned by other hands. Get the words out; stock someone else's empty shelves. Pack your extra books up and head to your local thrift shop, school, used bookstore, and/or library. (Even if the library can't use the volume on its shelves, it will probably welcome your donation for its next used-book sale.)

The best way to sort your books for your shelves or for distribution is to separate them by category: novels, gardening, health, sports, hobbies, entertainment, music, science, travel, children's books. Be sure you have all books from all locations in one place when you do this. Then make a list of the titles in each category, and underline your favorites. (If you find yourself underlining every one, take a deep breath and start again.)

Now, don't go emotional on me. Get a grip. Once again, the moment of truth has arrived. All books with non-underlined titles go into several small, sturdy boxes (they get heavy in a hurry). Think happy thoughts: The books are reentering society to be seen through someone else's eyes, to have their pages flipped again rather than yellowing and growing musty. Let them go with grace, or cry a little if you need to. The sooner they are out of sight, the sooner they will be out of mind. The sooner the clutter will be gone. I know, it sounds demeaning to refer to a literary experience as clutter, but if it's been lying about unread, it's really just so much paper.

When you've finished placing the favorites on their shelves, evaluate the shelf space you now have available. Depending on the number of books you retrieved from other rooms, the shelves may be full. But if you do have some empty shelf space, hats off to you. Books look very happy when family photographs are placed next to them.

Ahh. You have successfully and dramatically cleared the clutter from the living areas of your home. You are now an official member of the clutter-buster patrol. A big responsibility, but you can handle it.

HOME OFFICE, DESK, COMMUNICATIONS CENTER and BILL PAYING

We are about to join forces, using our experience to link four areas that exist in your home (in one form or another) so that they will work together as one unit. The Helper Items for this section are available at any large office-supply store, or through the mail-order sources in Step Five, page 93.

1. **Large accordion file with 24 category pockets**—portable, can be dropped into a file drawer or stored in a closet.
2. **Small accordion file** for incoming mail.
3. **Portable file box.**
4. **Hanging file folders**—regular size.
5. **Labels for hanging and accordion files.**
6. **Bulletin board** for daily notes.
7. **Desktop note holder.**
8. **Pencils, pens, paperclips, rubber bands, and portable holder.**
9. **Notepaper holder** and **notepaper** in individual sheets.
10. **Address book.**
11. **Year-At-A-Glance** calendar.
12. **PDA (Personal Digital Assistant).**
13. **Letter opener.**
14. **Staple gun and staples.**
15. **Ruler.**
16. **Clear tape.**
17. **Envelopes**—blank and letterhead.
18. **Scissors.**
19. **Drawer organizer tray.**

We have conquered some big forces, brought down most of the wall of clutter. During the organization process, you've probably noticed that there is a mischievous culprit that's been colonizing your home. That would be The Piler. The Piler's ways seem harmless in the beginning—

just one or two bland sheets of paper—but as those sheets multiply and gang up, The Piler starts to become a Pilferer as well. When you're not looking, it seeks out lone pieces of paper to add to its stacks, determined to see how high it can go.

There is no Piler antibiotic, no exterminator. There is only one solution: to fight back. I know you've been thinking that, in due course, you would reduce each and every pile to a bare spot on the desk, on the bookshelf, on the floor. But you also know about best-laid plans, good intentions. You need to take positive action, right now, to keep those piles from shutting out the light, from stopping the circulation of air around your home, from cluttering your mind.

How do you win the war with The Piler for good? You methodically bring down each pile, selectively saving important documents, bills and statements, putting them into a file for safekeeping. So, are you ready? We are going to develop a strategic plan.

No war is won without the right equipment. The recommended Helper Items cost little to buy, but will make a huge contribution in corralling and taming the papers on your desk and in your office/bill paying/communications area(s). If your home has an office as a separate entity, congratulations! With an office, it's very easy to isolate papers and prevent pileups. Chances are you haven't been doing that—but you're about to start!

Let's go back into the living room, where those piles are anxiously awaiting their sentencing. Take a deep breath, and start sorting by category.

Active File Categories—Daily, Weekly, Monthly

Incoming mail
Unpaid bills
Bank statements/reconciled
Paid bills by category:
    Utilities
    Credit cards
    Mortgage, loans
    Medical
    Groceries

Home and cell phone
Insurance
Clothing
House maintenance
Sporting goods
Vehicle
Hobby
Education
Cash receipts
Property tax
Rent
Memberships
Contributions
Professional services
Brokerage, mutual fund statements

Inactive Files

Insurance policies
Insurance claims
Income tax data for current year
Vehicle service records
Appliance warrantees and instructions
Medical records
Children's education
Travel, frequent-flyer records
Religion
Retirement
Mortgage, loan agreements
Lease agreements
Legal and military records
Contracts
Household inventory
Miscellaneous

Birth certificates, passports, death certificates, marriage certificates, and divorce decrees should all be stored in a secure, fire-resistant safe. (You can find a recommendation in the Helper Items section.)

The war on paper begins at your door. Label the small accordion file Incoming Mail and locate it where you enter the house, at the back door or the front door. An accordion file offers the benefits of an extensive pocket system and the ability to expand without being cumbersome. It is also portable, which allows you to carry it to a comfortable area of your home when it comes time to manage your paperwork. Hold on, now. This isn't permission to start piling up the dining-room table again—although that surface does make a fine substitute desk, as long as you do your work and then Put It Back. That is all-important. If you don't want to relapse and fall right back into the clutter trap, you have to Put It all Back, even if you were unable to finish paying your bills in one session. You will be so proud of yourself once you get into the routine.

To keep your papers organized, you will need two file systems—one for active daily, weekly, and monthly filing, and one for inactive files. I would suggest an accordion file for the active and a portable file with a hard case for the inactive, unless you have a file cabinet. There are a total of 23 active file categories and 16 inactive categories. For the accordion file, print each category clearly on a sticker label, and affix. For the portable file, clearly print each inactive category on a hanging file label. Drop the folders into the portable holder.

Now that you have the labeling completed, but before we reduce your piles to zero, let's become acquainted with each file category. The accordion folder for **incoming mail** may be small, but it's very powerful—a titan that will not allow any incoming mail to get by, with one exception: **incoming bills**, which have their own designated file. They need to be separated for priority treatment, and kept in their holding area until payment day. Incoming bills should be dated on arrival, with a notation next to the incoming date of the date payment is due. (Most bills have a due date listed, but it's best for your mind processor to record both dates at once. That will automatically set up your memory-reminder system.)

Bank statements: Consider paying bills online if you are not already doing so. It is easy, efficient, and saves time. All banks now have online bill-paying systems, and they all function basically the same. Once you go through the setup, you have only to log on, enter your password, pull up your balance, and enter the bills you want paid. There is still a manual aspect to this process, in that most bills will continue to be mailed to your home and you will be trapping them on entry, posting the arrival and due date, and filing them in the unpaid bill file. The online process does eliminate paper statements, though, along with canceled checks and reconciliation. Your complete statement status comes up on the computer screen, listing checks deposited, debits, bank charges, and balance. You may want to go on receiving paper statements for the first couple of months until you are comfortable with the new procedure, but I recommend you discontinue them after that.

Now that you have a fix on the how-to of better bill paying, let's get back to your filing system. Having individual categories for quick referral back to **paid bills** saves time throughout the year, and provides quick access when gathering receipts for tax returns. Paid bills—properly marked with the date paid and the check or reference number—are retired, at rest, and no longer imbued with any urge to torment or irritate you. They are, however, likely to sulk and hide if they are not filed properly in their assigned folder. If that happens, I can assure you, there will be problems—with the potential for yet another internal paper war. Put Them Back where they belong, and you'll know where to find them.

If you receive a monthly or quarterly **brokerage or mutual fund statement**, place it in its file as soon as it comes in the door. Unless you are an active investor with monthly transactions, these statements don't require much review time. If your broker or mutual fund provides a complete online service, you can review your status online each month and eliminate the paper review. Not receiving a hard copy at home could completely eliminate this file category; but the decision depends on how comfortable you are with your broker.

Remember, while inactive files may be second string, they are important—and you never know when they will be called upon to play a role in your life. They should always be healthy and ready to perform. A folder holding your **insurance policies** may be boring, but you've got to have one. Same for **insurance claims**.

Part of managing your time at the beginning of each calendar year is starting a new folder for **income tax** data. Any receipts that apply to your tax return should go into this folder, from the closing statement on a piece of property you sold, to the check from a restaurant where you had a business lunch.

It's a good idea to have your **vehicle** serviced following the manufacturer's recommended maintenance schedule. This keeps the car operating efficiently and wards off mechanical failure. It's also a good idea to keep the service records handy in your own file system. If your dealer has a good follow-up procedure and record-maintenance program, you may be able to eliminate this file category, but only if you are confident that they will follow through and remind you when your car is due for service.

Appliance warrantees and instructions can amount to a stack, and might require more than one folder. This is an important category, since we often have to refer back to operating instructions for appliances—and if anything goes wrong, you'll be very happy to know just where the warranty is. (Keep the sales receipt clipped to the warranty, for easy reference to and proof of the purchase date.) Also, if you decide to sell your home, this information will be important to the new prospective owner.

Managing our health is a major part of our lives. Keep a complete file of **medical records** for all members of the household, including dental appointments and procedures, vision exams and corrections, and visits to dermatologists and other specialists.

The other file categories are self-explanatory, with the possible exception of **household inventory**. I encourage you to create a detailed list of all of the contents of your home, along with their value. If you're not sure of the value, obtain an estimate from an assessor, do your own research, or give it your best-shot estimate. Once this list is complete, you'll have a comprehensive record for any future insurance claims due to fire or theft. It should be kept in your fire-resistant **Brinks safe**, along with any items you find in your piles that should be secured. Reminder—the safe should contain at least your family's birth, marriage and death certificates, passports, wills, divorce decrees, cash, rare collections, and expensive, special-occasion jewelry.

It's time for the files to knock out the piles. You are all set up, ready to sort through the captives corralled in the holding area, waiting and confused. Bring along a heavy-duty plastic bag so you can trash all the junk mail and useless coupons, articles you don't really want to read, subscriptions you no longer want to renew, old invitations and holiday cards, and old or uninteresting catalogs (unless they are recyclable in your area).

File any paid bills from previous years in a manila envelope labeled with the year. Separate all current paid bills by category, and drop them into their slots in the accordion file. The rest is easy. Continue dropping papers into the appropriate files until all of the piles have been vanquished and you have won the war on paper clutter—cleared the deck, cleared your mind. Now for the finish.

Where do your new files go? If you have an office or a desk, the ideal place would be in a file cabinet or drawer. (Review the list of Helper Items to make sure you're covered.) A closet can be used as a storage area for files, but only after it has been reorganized and you know what it contains. If closet space is limited and you have no office or desk, we have to find you a place to store your files. End-table cabinets are listed in the Helper Items section. Other options are a narrow, upright desk or a lift-top ottoman. Keep in mind that what we are doing is basically consolidation, regardless of the size of your home. We're eliminating what you don't need and reducing what you do need down to its simplest functional form, so that it works well in your environment.

Our job is done here. Much of what you have learned in organizing your home office area will also be useful in your workplace.

THE LAUNDRY ROOM

The Helper Items you'll need for organizing your laundry room can be found in the mail-order source section, Step Five, page 95.

1. **Combination ironing board/iron hanger.**
2. **Spring-expansion rod** for hanging clothes to be ironed.
3. **Standing rack** for hanging clothes that require line drying.
4. **Wall shelf unit** for supplies if cabinets are not available.
5. **Laundry basket.**
6. **Trash basket** for dryer lint.

All laundry rooms serve the same purpose, regardless of size; but when it comes to folding and ironing, the larger the better. If you do have a large laundry room but don't have a hanging combo ironing board/iron holder, this is the time to get one. Or, if you want to trade up and you have the wall space, treat yourself to a folding ironing board that installs like a cabinet. All of these are listed in Helper Items, along with a hanging rod for clothes.

If your laundry area is in a large closet or is barely more than the size of one, it can still be an adequate, functional space. You probably have enough room on one side to hang a combo ironing board/iron holder. The space above the washer and dryer may have room for a spring-loaded hanging rod, but if this space is occupied with cabinets or shelves (perfect for detergents and supplies), install a simple hanging rod that folds back flat against the wall or cabinet when not in use. If there are no cabinets or shelves but space is available, you can purchase a wall unit to hold detergents and supplies (see Helper Items). Even if you have a stacked washer/dryer in a tiny closet, there may still be room to hang an ironing board/iron holder; and detergents and supplies can be stored neatly on top of the dryer.

Laundry closets have the tendency to accumulate dryer lint and dust, so they need a vac-zap periodically. They also have the potential to be out-of-control clutter-breeding areas, collecting piles of dirty laundry that build until they are scattered by someone searching for a piece of clothing that's gone "missing." If they're left long enough, those piles can also send out less than pleasant odors to infiltrate adjoining rooms of your house. If your nose is out of joint from the dirty-laundry sniff, there's a very easy solution. Unlike piles of paper, which seem to have a will to survive and multiply, piles of laundry want to disappear. They don't like the way they feel or smell. They'd jump into the suds on their own if they could—but they need your help.

It's important to have respect for the clothes we wear even when they are in the dirty-laundry state. They shouldn't be chucked haphazardly into a musty pile just because they've served their purpose for the day. That's mean, so get them clean. Keep them happy and fresh, and they will keep you snappy. Doing laundry as soon as you have a load is part of Putting It Back. Keep clearing the clutter, clearing your mind.

LINEN CLOSET

No Helper Items are required.

Linen closets are generally located near bedrooms. In a small, apartment-style environment, the linen closet may be in the master bedroom or near the main living area. If that's the case with yours, it's all too likely become a catchall for the overload from the bedrooms and bathrooms. Relocating useful items shouldn't pose much of a problem at this stage, since we have already been through those rooms and have created plenty of space.

Go through the usual elimination process in the linen closet, removing everything from the shelves. Anything that is no longer being used should go. Keep only enough extra linens for guests. Even things that have been handed down through your family (unless you really care about them and have found a use for them) should be passed on. When you are finished with the elimination process, you should have extra room for placemats, napkins, silverware, and even (if you have no other option) file folders. You may also want to use some of this reclaimed storage space for bulk items like paper towels and toilet paper, but only if you have no room for them in the kitchen or bathroom.

POWDER ROOM

The Helper Items you'll need for organizing your powder room can be found in the mail-order source section, Step Five, page 95.

1. Hand-towel rack or ring.
2. Tissue holder.
3. Candles.
4. Soap dish.
5. Trash pail.

If you have a medium-size or larger home, you probably have a mid-size powder room. In a small home with limited space, a bathroom shared with a bedroom usually does double-duty as a powder room. Either way, there shouldn't be much clutter, since we've already organized any shared bathrooms, and very little time is spent in a designated powder room. So just spiff it up a bit, and you're there.

FRONT-ENTRY and BACKDOOR CLOSETS

Helper Items for organizing these closets can be found in the mail-order source section in Step Five, page 95.

1. Hangers.
2. Hanging vacuum-cleaner tool caddy.
3. Dust buster.
4. Duster, broom, dustpan.
5. Wall brackets for cleaning tools.
6. Hanging hat rack.

The number of closets in your home will determine how you use your front-entry closet. Ideally, it should be used only for guests' outerwear; but this is hardly a reality in most homes. If closet space is limited, the front entry tends to bear the burden of the overflow: whatever doesn't fit anywhere else ends up there. If you have a backdoor closet as well, it should be the designated area for your outerwear, boots, gloves, bags, and umbrellas. It can also work in combination as a utility closet—a home for your vacuum and accessories, dusters, brooms, etc. If you have no backdoor closet, you'll probably have to keep a few of your outer garments and accessories in the front-entry closet. It's balancing act. How you divide the space should be based on your lifestyle and the frequency with which you have guests.

With the recommended Helper Items, you can easily set up either closet so it is clutter-free and everything you need is in sight. The front and back entries provide first and last impressions of your home, for guests and for residents. When you leave your home in the morning, you probably take a last-minute glance around—and that is the impression of your home you carry with you. In the same way, your first glimpse inside your home at the end of the day makes an impression that will influence the way you feel for the rest of the evening.

Take advantage of a vicarious lesson from my cousin Al, the King of Clutter, who had to learn the hard way to renounce his "throne" and abdicate as ruler of his pile-building kingdom. When the towers by his back door slid into the narrow pathway he had been using to go in and out, he switched to using the front door—and, of course, leaving new piles there whenever he possibly could. When those piles slid to the floor, probably because the cat had brushed by, cousin Al was at work. He had to brace his feet against the porch railing and push—hard—with his shoulder to get in.

Don't be like Al. Whether you enter your home through the front door or the back door, you need to feel good about your pad, your digs, the place you call home. It represents who you are, and its entry points have to be clutter free. Open and clear.

ATTIC and BASEMENT

Helper Items for organizing the attic and basement can be found in the mail-order source section in Step Five, page 96.

1. **Cedar and canvas clothes-storage closet** or **jumbo storage bag.**
2. **Open plastic shelving.**
3. **Clear plastic storage boxes.**

If you have an attic or basement or both, the odds are you've been using these places to hide the overload. You've hidden away old "treasures" you just couldn't throw away at the time (how long ago?), thinking you'd get back to them one day, get them sorted out. Sure, sure. We all know that one: "Out of sight, out of mind." This stuff has been out of sight for so long, you probably don't even remember you have it. And if you can't remember it, how can you possibly need it? Of course, you may be emotionally attached to certain memorabilia— old family photographs and portraits, old toys and games, perhaps some heirloom linens or antique furniture you would like to pass on to someone. Well, the time has come to pass it on.

Even if you rarely take notice of them, your attic and basement are part of your home's periphery. You're releasing yourself from the world of clutter, so be sure these remote areas are clear, too. If you let them turn into clutter caves that are unpleasant and perhaps somewhat dangerous to enter, you might avoid them altogether except when opening the door to cram in more of the overload. The stuff inside may never see the light of day until you decide to move. All too often, that's what people do: they rid themselves of years of attic and basement collecting when they move. We don't want that for you. We want you clutter free, inside and out.

So, let's finish the job, do it right. The same principles we've used elsewhere apply here. If you don't use it, get rid of it. Decide which pieces of memorabilia you really want to keep, and pass the rest on to other family members or friends who might have the perfect use for these things, or the perfect place to display them. Once the overload has been banished, get out the vacuum and give these spaces a good going-over. This would also be a great time for a quick brighten-up with a light-colored paint. Make your basement or attic a place you might actually want to visit on occasion.

Use the recommended Helper Items to further organize these spaces and put them to good use. The portable cedar/canvas closet or the jumbo storage bag now has the perfect place to stay while holding your seasonal clothing—and you'll be able to access it easily when the time comes. Install simple, lightweight plastic shelving to hold clear plastic storage boxes—small, medium, and large. Here is the home for those Christmas decorations, and for your luggage when you're not traveling.

Your attic and basement are now functional places that will work in harmony with your primary living areas. You are managing the space around you, paving the way toward managing your time and gaining those two extra hours a day.

THE GARAGE

The following Helper Items can make a big difference in getting your garage organized. They can be found in the mail-order source section, Step Five, page 96.

1. **Wall-mounted pet food dispenser.** (Alternatively, use a large **plastic pail** that fits conveniently into a corner.)
2. **Pulley-suspended bicycle hanger**—allows you to pull your bike or bikes up to the ceiling easily for storage, and let them gently down to the floor when needed. (As an alternative, **ceiling or wall hooks** can be used to hang the bikes.)
3. **Storage rack** for soccer balls, footballs, tennis and golf balls, base balls, bats, mitts, tennis racquets. (**Wall hooks** are an option for hanging the bats, mitts, racquets, and for hanging **wire baskets** to hold the balls.)
4. **Five-station wall tool hanger**—a very simple way to keep all of your tools in one place and easily accessible.
5. **Storage racks**—ceiling-mounted versions work well if you have wasted ceiling space. Otherwise, standing shelving units can contain storage boxes and miscellaneous items.
6. **Stepladder.**
7. **Recycling bins** for paper, glass, cans, and (if applicable) plastic. (Alternatively, call your city or town hall to see what they offer for free.)
8. **Garden caddy on wheels**—has the potential to hold every tool for the job. (**Wall hooks** will keep garden tools organized and out of the way, although you will have to remember to Put Them Back.)

Is your garage a funky place? Is it burdened, overstuffed—possibly even too cluttered for you to squeeze your car inside?

If you think of your garage as an unimportant space, a sort of catchall to hold whatever doesn't have a place in the house, think again. Your waking day begins and ends in the bedroom, but your workday actually begins and ends in the garage.

After I went through my organizational process inside the house, I discovered that something was missing when I returned home at the end of the day. The visual and emotional impact when I drove into my crowded garage was disturbing, and it seemed that my good, productive day was ending in a lazy, hazy evening. I felt like I was being pulled down. With the usual garage clutter all around me on the walls, ceiling, and floor, I felt surrounded—almost as if I were in a slightly menacing forest with strange creatures all around, about to move when I wasn't looking.

Then, one day, a revelation came over me: The experience of entering the garage should be the same as when entering my home through the front door—inviting and warm, saying, "Come on in." The garage should offer the same welcoming feeling you want your guests to have when visiting, and it should be a reflection of who you are, what you are about.

Of course, you can't accomplish this to the same degree in the garage as in the foyer. But you can eliminate the garage clutter and relieve your eyes of that "what you see is what you get" impression.

Organizing my garage was a challenge, but a worthy one. Thinking of it as another room, an actual part of the house, I became an interior garage designer. When the process was complete, I hung some artwork to give myself something wonderful to look at, and to help the space feel more like a room. From then on, when I was leaving home in the morning to begin my workday, I walked to my car with a light heart. And when I returned at the end of the day, it was a relief to know that I was going into a relaxed environment. No clutter, no stress. Even the cars seemed happier.

The garage is now a place where I like to hang out, do hobbies and repairs. It's part of my home. You may not want to go to this extreme, but try out the thought process anyway. Consider what you see when you arrive home, and the emotional impact it has.

Remember my illustration about the conscious and subconscious mind at work? When you arrive home, you consciously want to get into the house, often in a rushed and anxious way. But why? Your subconscious may be disturbed, without your being aware of it. You may be suppressing your dissatisfaction with being in the garage even for those few minutes, and may feel only a pressing need to get into the house and relax. The subconscious won't be happy if the conscious is in denial, doesn't want to deal with what it is seeing, and a battle will begin between the two. In the morning, you're likely to put the blinders on and make a ten-second dash for the car, rushing out into the world as quickly as possible. The subconscious may be whispering, "Hey, when are you going to stop avoiding what you're really feeling, and do something about this mess?" That was the story with me—and when my sub finally took charge, I gave myself a great "front-entry garage."

One thing is for sure: You don't want to live like Bert and Sandy, who parked outside their garage for two years. Sandy was a collector, a triple-A athlete at buying stuff. The fun was always in the hunt. If she heard of a sale, no matter where it was, Sandy would show up and track her quarry. Yard sales were her passion and became her expertise. No one wanted to mess with Sandy when she was in killer mode. When she got out of her car at a yard sale, folks cringed and tried not to notice her, but that was like trying not to notice a bull that was being released from the pen. Sandy never walked away without goring, and always for the lowest price.

The only problem (other than the occasional infestation of mice) was Bert, who was not cut from the same fabric. Bert could not stand clutter, never bought anything he didn't need, and if he'd had something for more than a year and hadn't used it, he got rid of it —if, that is, he could find it under his wife's piles of "collectibles." He had tried to talk to Sandy many times about the garage—how much he missed being able to use his workbench, and how much he hated parking in the street—and Sandy had promised many times that she would sort through each box and bag and either put the items to good use or organize them for her own Yard Sale of Yard Sales. Unfortunately, her days off from work were the same weekend days she felt compelled to spend hunting for more stuff . . . and time kept slipping away.

After two years of scraping ice off his car's windshield in winter and repeatedly washing bird droppings off the hood in summer, and after a week of evenings spent fruitlessly searching for his favorite adjustable wrench, Bert decided to take the garage into his own hands. Driven to recklessness by frustration, he was determined to reclaim his workbench. One Saturday, when he thought Sandy was going to be at her sister's for the entire day, he had a dumpster delivered to their house.

Bert planned get rid of things that were damaged, useless, or hadn't seen the light of day in years, while saving Sandy's real treasures and stacking them neatly on her side of the garage. He could hardly wait to find the walls, and was filled with anticipation at the thought of finally being able to park his car in the garage again. He felt confident that he could pull this caper off and that Sandy would forgive him when she saw what a wonderful job he'd done. Things were going well until he was carrying his last load out of the garage, and Sandy suddenly appeared.

There were no words to express Sandy's range of emotion when she saw her world unraveling, coming apart in front of her. Her blood pressure rose from her toes to her nose. Her hands were shaking. She felt that the only way she could save herself was to save her stuff. Muttering at Bert, she used the burst of adrenaline to jump into the giant dumpster, now half full of several years' worth of "trophies." She proceeded to throw each and every one of them out into the driveway, remembering the kill date of all.

Bert didn't know what to do. What he did know was that if he valued his life, he had to get out of the line of fire, so he found a spot behind a tree trunk, in the shade. He was beginning to think he'd been overly optimistic in anticipating Sandy's forgiveness.

As Sandy began to recover from the initial shock, she began flinging words out of the dumpster along with her rescued possessions. A neighbor walking by couldn't help but observe that Bert was conversing with a dumpster that seemed to be throwing kinky garden hoses, plywood Halloween decorations, and gap-toothed wicker chairs in his direction, missing him by inches. As the "conversation" continued, Sandy accused Bert of being mentally unbalanced. She told him he needed therapy and she would arrange for it. Bert's response was, "Sandy, I'm not the one who's mentally unbalanced; you're the packrat in the dumpster."

Bert and Sandy ended up settling their differences. Both compromised. Sandy found things to do on the weekends other than shop madly for the deal of the century. Bert taped a line down the center of the garage, separating "his" side from "hers"—and promised NEVER again to throw away anything of Sandy's without permission. He was much happier with his car parked out of the weather, his tools accessible, and his golf clubs out of hiding. And, after enough time had gone by that Sandy could feel sure that she wasn't doing it because of pressure from Bert, she did organize her stuff—hanging, mounting, framing, storing, giving away, and, yes, selling a couple of real deals at a tidy profit. They are considering taking the drastic measure of removing the tape from the garage floor.

The garage tends to bear the brunt of our daily lives. It's where we empty the car, get a little lazy, and neglect to carry the daily catch any further. It's catch-as-catch-can. But . . . don't worry; be happy. You can change your ways, and you can make your garage someplace you like to be.

So, pick a clear day, pull all of that stuff out of the garage, line it up according to what you (really) do and do not need, and sell, give, or throw away every last thing on the "not" side. When you are finished, refer to the Helper Items to assist you in the organizational process. Select what you think will work for you, and don't opt out of the recycling bins. They'll help you clear the clutter daily, while keeping recyclables out of the landfill. Up, up, and away . . .

YOUR CAR AND TRUNK

Helper Items needed for organizing the car and trunk can be found in the mail-order source section, Step Five, page 97.

1. **Coat or jacket hanger**—perfect for keeping that jacket neat for work. Hangs on the back of the front seat and does not obstruct the driver's view. Alternatively, use a regular coat hanger.
2. **Lap desk**—ideal for the office on wheels. Very convenient and comfortable for getting work done when taking a break from driving.
3. **Seat-back organizer**—for extra CDs, cassettes, games, and maps. This is suggested only if you travel with a large collection and all internal seat pockets are being used.
4. **Trash container.** If you spend a lot of time in your car, trash will collect—so have a designated place to keep it contained.
5. **Clothes hanging bar**—will hold enough for a two-person road trip. Hanging clothes will stay neat and unwrinkled, saving you time.
6. **Trunk organizer**—for tools and cleaning solutions.
7. **Glove compartment organizer**—an insert that provides separate compartments for driver registration/insurance card, extra keys, pens/pencils, tissues, owner's manual, parking pass. No more fumbling.

Unless you are a parent of young children and therefore subject to chauffeur duty on a daily basis, your car is a personal chamber, a space where you spend private time while being transported from one location to the next. Whether you're driving to work or for pleasure, for those minutes or hours, you are by yourself, focused on your driving but aware of the music or the news broadcast. It's an environment where you can allow your subconscious and conscious to think constructively.

You probably selected your car because you enjoy the way it feels, the way it drives, the way it provides security while transporting you to your destination. Whether you spend ten minutes, an hour, or several hours at a time driving, the car is your comfort zone. You want it to be there for you—and, like you, it has to be cared for so that it is healthy and dependable. Servicing on the recommended manufacturer's schedule will keep your car ready and at peak performance, so it will never let you down.

Like your home, the car can be a clutter collector. Its doors are open to all that you let in: mail, newspapers, magazines, packages, clothing, shoes, pet stuff, kid stuff, miscellaneous food and drink containers.

Although Vinny ate a lot of meals on the road, the only time the interior of his car received any attention was when he took his lady friend, Linda, out for dinner. Most of the time he was late picking her up because he always underestimated how long it would take him to get his car to the point where it wasn't an embarrassment. One day, however, Vinny picked Linda up for a day of shopping, and he was on time. She was so impressed with the immaculate car that she didn't even have the urge to protect her skirt from potential potato-chip crumbs by wiping off the seat before sliding in.

The hours-long shopping mission yielded many packages, and Linda insisted for security reasons that they should be stashed in the trunk. In the midst of Vinny's confusing explanation as to why that might not be a good idea, Linda said, "Oh, don't be silly," and popped the trunk open. And there was the reason Vinny had been on time—mounds of clutter hiding in darkness. While Vinny hid his red face behind armloads of packages, Linda made several trips to the parking garage's trash receptacle. Vinny vowed that from that day on, he would not allow even a gum wrapper to spend the night in his car. And he and Linda lived happily ever after.

Your car needs to be free—free of random objects, free of clutter. When you open that door in the morning, you don't want to look at last week's mail, a half-empty water bottle, and pens and pencils stuck in the beverage holder. There should be no notes, old or new, hanging off the sun visors. Your car should be an extension of your home. If it is clutter free, your mind can be clear to perform and deliver the feedback you need in your private time on the road.

Clutter is a creeper. It creeps in wherever and whenever we allow it. Ask yourself, "Do I know for sure where my current car registration and insurance card are? Are they in a secure container in the glove compartment, readily accessible without sorting through papers from previous years?" If your car has a CD player, is the CD compartment overloaded with mail, doctors' prescriptions, directions? When you pull down your sun visor, is there any chance you'll find a wedding

61

invitation you didn't answer on time? Are the side-door pockets filled with snack food wrappers? Is the trunk full of sporting gear, tools, clothes you meant to drop off last season at the dry cleaners?

If so, get into clutter-buster mode. Remove the trash. Sort out any important mail, placing it in the appropriate file in your office. Recycle any old reading material. Put clothing and shoes back where they belong (or put them into a laundry bag and take them to the cleaners *today*). Collect all extra pens and pencils.

Open the glove compartment and remove what is not needed or is outdated, leaving your current registration and insurance card in a proper, secure envelope. Your car owner's manual belongs here as well—but that's about all. The glove compartment is a natural for catching it all (even gloves!) behind a closed door—"Oh, I'll just stuff it there for now and take it out later." Sure, we all know that one. And we all know that in those (perhaps tense) moments when you do have to find that registration card, it can be a dandy of a challenge. Being organized is being ready.

Open the trunk and remove any sports equipment, placing it in its assigned space in the garage. This will keep the equipment in good condition, at the ready, clean and undamaged. You'll always know where to find it when you need it.

If you don't carry the habit of Putting It Back with you out to your car, no matter how clear of clutter your home is now, you are still vulnerable. The car can pull you down, back into being a collector again. Release your car from clutter, and you will both be smiling, ready to go.

BACKDOOR MUDROOM and ENTRY

Helper Items for organizing your backdoor mudroom and entry can be found in the mail-order source section, Step Five, page 97.

1. **Jacket/coat wall hanger.**
2. **Boot and sport-shoe rack.**
3. **Umbrella stand.**
4. **Doormat.**
5. **Key rack.**

The mudroom should exude the same welcoming warmth as the front entry. Entering your home should always feel good and be visually pleasing, even from the back door.

Apply the same process you've already been through in your closets. Everything should be organized and have its own place.

If your mudroom has old, inactive stuff in it—out of style, doesn't fit—it's out of there. Keep only what you really need. If you already have a boot and shoe rack, a coat and jacket rack, and a doormat, all you have to do is make sure everything is clean and in good working order. If not, new ones are a cinch to install, along with a key rack. Label your keys and hang them in place.

This space is easy to keep clean and clutter-free, but you have to be consistent. It is all too easy to just kick off your boots and leave them, especially if your hands are full of groceries or a load of wood. It's also tempting to bring the recycling only as far as the mudroom, telling yourself, "Tomorrow"—but tomorrow, as they say, never comes; and who wants to trip over heavy boots and bags of bottles and cans day after day?

Please don't be fooled by the name "mudroom"—it is not an indication that this is the place to store mud. If you kick off the crud and leave it, this will not be a pleasant entry to your home for long. And that crud has thousands of little ways to hitch a ride all through the house. You want your mudroom to be bright and clean, with good light—maybe even some outdoor family photos, or fishing and hunting shots. Just because you don't spend much time here doesn't mean it's unimportant. You want to feel good, not discouraged, when you pass through.

TRASH PAILS

The Helper Item section has a wide variety of trash pails. You can find them in the mail-order source section in Step Five, page 98.

Surprisingly, one of the biggest battles against clutter can take place in your trash pails. Most are out of sight, where you can ignore them; but quiet clutter knows the element of surprise, and you have to know how to manage it if you want to avoid Trash Trauma. Even if all of your trash pails are under cover, behind cabinet doors, you still have to look at them every time you open that door to make a deposit. If you clear the clutter in the rest of your home but allow overflowing trash pails, you are still allowing your eyes and mind to be clobbered by clutter.

The rule is, when the trash reaches within a few inches of the rim, it's ready to be emptied. The way to manage this most efficiently and with the least amount of balking is to have each pail lined with a plastic bag. It's easier and less time-consuming to remove each bag from each location, tie them and take them to the main trash can than it is to take each pail out and dump it individually. This method also keeps crud from accumulating on the sides of the pail.

To help you clear the clutter, you should have trash pails in the laundry room, bedrooms, bathrooms, office, den, and garage. Kitchen trash is a different species.

If your home has a garbage disposal, 98 percent of your waste food can be disposed of that way. Cans and bottles (and, where allowed, recyclable plastic containers) should be rinsed and placed in recycling. This reduces your kitchen trash to mostly paper and non-recyclable plastic, which can be crushed by hand before depositing in the trash pail, saving time by reducing the number of emptying trips.

Trash compactors can be handy, but beware. When Mary bought a new home, one of the features that sold her on it was the trash compactor—and she did love using it. The only problem was removing the full bags, which weighed more than Mary. Typical of trash compactors, hers obligingly swallowed everything she fed it, until it was full and overfull. Fortunately for Mary, her neighbor could have doubled for the Incredible Hulk, and he was happy to help with the removal process—at least for the first few times. After that, Mary realized it was time for the trash compactor to go on a diet.

If you don't have a garbage disposal, you'll need a trash pail with a tightly sealed lid to keep odors from escaping. (Even better, think about investing in a composter to set in an out-of-the-way corner of your yard, and use a compost bucket with a filter in the kitchen. Your lawn and flowers will thank you.) It's very important to remove waste food frequently. Even with a tightly sealed lid, anaerobic conditions can promote some unsightly—and very unpleasant-smelling—molds in just a few days, and your nose will start complaining that something needed to be done yesterday.

Stay with the program. Don't put off trash management for another day, another week. If you follow the rule—almost level to the top and bag it—you will have a happy trash day, and no more clutter. Have trash, will travel.

THE PURSE or WALLET,
THE SHOULDER BAG or BRIEFCASE

Helper Items can be found in the mail-order source section, page 98.

1. Woman's shoulder bag.
2. Purse.
3. Woman's wallet.
4. Man's money clip.
5. Briefcase.
6. Man's wallet.

It's been said countless times over the centuries: "Men and women are different." Yes, they are, and that's a good thing. But, especially today, there is more than one common thread in how men and women conduct their everyday lives.

When they leave home in the morning, both are dressed and prepared for the day in clothing that represents who they are and how they feel about themselves—their taste and style. And they carry similar "support systems" to get them through the day—a purse or a wallet. These functional and necessary items are like our clothing . . . can't leave home without them, or without the things they carry— credit cards, business cards, driver's license, insurance card, photos, club card, parking card, Social Security card, notes.

The contents of the purse or the wallet are referred to and accessed numerous times throughout the day, and it can be difficult and time-consuming to find what you're looking for if the "system" is overloaded.

Simpler, lighter, and easier systems are available, and I'm going to recommend a different concept. It will be a change, but remember: modifying the way you do certain things can make your life less stressful.

For women, I recommend a hanging pouch to replace the purse, and for men, a money clip to replace the wallet. Now, hang on . . . I know you're thinking, "How am I supposed to fit all of that stuff in a smaller space?" And the answer is, you're not. These two systems are designed to contain only the essentials for any given day—two or three credit cards and a driver's license. You'll be reducing the weight you carry every day by ounces, or even pounds.

Have you ever carried a purse so full that it was barely able to reach the critical threshold of closure, so solid with stuff you were afraid to throw it over your shoulder for fear it might slam into your ribcage like a ramming ball? While that could be to a woman's advantage in a confrontation with a mugger, it's better to leave the lethal-weapon-size bag at home and travel light, avoiding potential mugging situations altogether.

Then there is the bulging wallet most men carry in their back pocket. Not very comfortable when you sit down—although, after it's been sat on enough, your wallet will obligingly take on the shape of your butt. Real flattering when you pull it out. And when you attempt to open it, the contents have been pressed into a corresponding contour, packed so tightly you need to drive a wedge through the side to get it to spring loose. (On the up side, at least you don't have to be worried about anything falling out.)

Shoulder bags and briefcases far outweigh the average purse or wallet, becoming a home away from home and carrying enough stuff to keep you occupied if you become stranded on an island for a week. There was a time when either would hang comfortably from the shoulder, but they have become so heavy that they are a danger to the skeletal structure. It's not unusual for them to weigh between 10 and 15 pounds, jammed with calculators, pens, pencils, paperclips, books, a PDA, an extra sweater, stamps, folders, business cards, notepaper, appointment book, envelopes, aspirin, rubber bands, ruler, sewing kit, reading glasses, cell phone, band-aids, keys, snack food and/or lunch, newspaper, and magazines. Sounds like something a bona-fide bag person would carry.

I have a hunch you've figured out where we're heading with this. Yes. Change and action are about to occur. I want you to talk yourself out of your old bag of tricks, and into what is about to happen.

Organization and mind-clearing are journeys, not destinations. But we are reaching the end of the clutter-busting process, with most areas free. Your daily hands-on support system is about to be freed as well, taking on a new look, a new style, a new way to be there for you. Once it is released from the clutches of clutter, your "baggage" will perform well for you each day—a world-class performance, with Kentucky Derby swiftness and New York City Ballet grace.

Ask yourself, "How much of what I carry each day do I actually need?" Think simplicity, think implementation.

Begin with your purse and/or wallet. Remove all contents. Evaluate all credit cards. Take a moment for a reality check. Why carry so many? Have you added up the annual fees? (Sure, there are "free" ones in the collection, but having them is unnecessary, and contributes to overspending.) You need only a no-annual-fee Visa and MasterCard, both accepted all over the world. You probably have store credit cards, gas station credit cards, private club cards, and the biggest culprit creating card overload—the several bankcards you stuck into your wallet when they arrived, unsolicited, in the mail. The justification for having so many is to have more lines of credit, but there is really no need. All you have to do is ask your preferred bank for a credit-line increase. So—go, go, go. Pick your favorite bank, preferably one that provides frequent-flyer miles or free travel on the airline of your choice.

Do you also carry a bank debit card? Many people use a debit card for purchases because they are concerned about too many charges on their credit card, but that does not always reflect realistic thinking. Money is money. It doesn't matter what card is used to spend it; it still has to be accounted for. If you are depositing money in your checking account and using the debit card for sales transactions, you are still spending it, only faster, as it is deducted immediately from your checking account balance. It's time for smart spending. If you have credit card debt that you're carrying from month to month, paying high interest, the debit card could temporarily come in handy while you clear the debt. No need to carry more than one card, though, since the one with the debt load should be placed in a drawer and not see the light of day until the "Finance Charges" on your statement read $0.00.

Be tenacious in sending your mind the right messages, and be the master of your money. You are your own person. If you've been allowing external conditions to push you around, it's time to take control. Credit card debt can't be allowed to dictate what you do and how you make your decisions.

You can put yourself where you want to be, in charge of your life, by managing your time and the space around you. By being consistent. Part of smart spending is managing your finances, knowing exactly what your income and expenses are each month, and spending less than you bring in. It's an extension of managing your time and the space around you to stay balanced, able to avoid impulse purchases. As you become more efficient, it will seem silly that you ever thought you needed all of those credit cards.

It's time for a change—the change you've been wanting to make. Remember, you're not changing who you are; you're changing the way you do things.

If you're a woman, from Helper Items, select a shoulder bag with compartments for file folders, keys, extra change, cosmetics, receipts, a pen, a small notepad, PDA if you have one, a small day planner, a small packet of tissues, and a hairbrush. The bag should also have slots for business cards and one extra credit card, as well as a large slot to contain a thin wallet for your insurance cards, buying club and warehouse membership cards, Social Security card, health and athletic club cards, airline club cards, frequent-flyer cards, and—if it suits you—a small selection of family photos. All of these can remain in the shoulder bag slots, ready for easy access when you need them.

In addition, from Helper Items or from your favorite store, purchase a small purse with a thin shoulder strap and with no more than eight slots—to be used for two credit cards, emergency insurance card, driver's license, parking pass, club pass, and a few personal business cards. You now have a shoulder-bag-and-purse team that will function together to help keep you organized.

The plan is simple: The small purse makes a home in your shoulder bag. When you go shopping, to lunch or dinner, to meet friends, or to a business meeting, the shoulder bag stays behind. You carry just the small purse, holding your keys, touch-up cosmetics, hairbrush, any extra cards needed that day, PDA or small notepad. You are light and lively. Your shoulder bag is carrying the load, backing you up. When you have meeting to attend, it will be there, ready to assist.

So, what have we accomplished? We have eliminated the ramming-ball purse and created a functional, two-part bag system in which everything has its place. No more wasted minutes spent looking for lost keys, lipstick, sunglasses, or pens. Everything is accessible, ready to keep you organized and save you time. It's in the bag. You are good to go, with no stress, no rush. Lightening the load lightens the mind and straightens the spine.

If you're a man, the jammed, sculptured wallet has probably been with you for many years. Like carrying a pocketknife as a teenager, or wearing a certain baseball cap, your wallet probably became a habit with you in your early years. Everything you need is stuffed in there—or at least you think it is. Money, credit cards, insurance cards, club cards, driver's license, ATM card, Social Security card, business cards, several photos and notes, maybe even extra keys to the car and the back door.

What I am about to suggest may sound radical, but it's just part of the letting-go process. We're about to make a change that will finally allow you to sit down comfortably. Ready?

Lose the wallet. You don't need it. The only essentials for everyday use are a Visa and MasterCard, and your driver's license. Clear the credit clutter: no more store cards, gas cards, extra bankcards. Yes, you do need an insurance card, ATM card, Social Security card, and perhaps a warehouse membership card, parking pass, or club card, but they don't need to be carried on your person at all times.

Even if your line of work doesn't require you to have a briefcase, you'll probably find it useful. (The Helper Items section lists sources.) The briefcase you choose should have compartments for file folders, and slots for business cards, extra credit cards, insurance cards, Social Security card, parking pass, club cards, photos, and a small notepad, as well as small pockets for keys, calculator, memo pad, stamps, and your PDA, day planner, or address book. Exterior pockets should be big enough for newspapers and magazines.

The briefcase, like the women's shoulder bag, is your backup, your support system. It will be standing tall, packed and ready to go whenever you are. You'll walk into meetings confident that you have everything you need. Your briefcase is your sidekick, your strategic assistant—and it will help you eliminate the wallet. That's right, it's time to let go.

Select a nice, flat money clip from Helper Items. In the money clip, stash your cash, driver's license, and two credit cards. That's all you need to carry in your pocket, unless you there is something else you've been carrying in your wallet that you need every day. If you use something one day a week, it doesn't require hauling around; it can stay in the briefcase the other six days, along with all other infrequently used items. They'll be there, waiting to be accessed by you, ready for action. And remember, don't let clutter accumulate in your briefcase!

If, in your lifestyle, a briefcase would only be extra baggage, you can still apply the same method, using a flat wallet to contain all backup items. You'll carry a money clip to hold cash, two credit cards, and your driver's license, and store the flat wallet at home or in the locked glove compartment of your car.

Your personal backup system is extremely important in managing your time and the space around you, perhaps even more important than parts of your home or office, because you must use it several times every day. It is the most active tangible in your daily life. You will not have cleared all the clutter in your mind until you clear it from your wallet and briefcase.

Harry, the same guy who fed the dog Wheaties in the morning because he kept the dog food near the cereal, repeatedly had embarrassing moments until he changed his ways. At one business meeting, he opened his briefcase and his daughter's glitter-festooned lunch bag fell out onto the table. It didn't do much for his professional image to have to dash back to the school, where his hungry daughter was disappointedly pulling Harry's quarterly reports out of her book bag.

Remember, everything you do to organize and manage the space around you is part of managing your time. They go together, and you can't have one without the other. When you are organized, you are always prepared for that special opportunity, the one you have been waiting for. It's Your Time.

WHERE YOU WORK

With your home, car, and personal backup system now organized, you are ready to take on your work environment—the place where you spend most of your time. Basically, everything we have covered in organizing the space where you live also applies to the place where you work.

Clear the clutter. It's there—in and on your desk, in the cabinets and file folders. Every occupation requires you to have some sort of office format, whether you are a business person who spends most of your day in an office, a salesperson who is in and out of the office, an attorney who spends many hours in courtrooms and consultation rooms, a doctor making frequent trips from the office to the hospital, a nurse, an accountant, a secretary, a truck driver with an office on wheels, a pharmacist, an educator, a real-estate broker or developer, an athletic coach, a contractor, a landscaper, an excavator, a stockbroker or investment manager, a banker, a pet kennel owner, a theater manager, a retailer, a concierge, a cleaning and maintenance manager, an interior designer or architect, a car dealer, a gas station owner, a mechanic, an airline pilot, a chauffeur or taxi driver, an artist, a woodworker or seamstress, a scientist, a computer engineer, a software developer . . .

You need a place where you can collect your thoughts at the

beginning, middle, and end of the day. As in the home, the process in your work environment starts with eliminating what you don't need. But first, step back and assess. Think outside the box. This space must be organized for you to excel at your career goals, to be the best you can be. It needs to be efficient, but comfortable. The walls, the floor, the colors, and the furniture must look and feel good to you.

We have come a long way since we started organizing the space in your home. The journey represents an enormous accomplishment, one that has prepared you to begin managing your time. As you approach this final part of Step Three, think of it as the last row of bricks being laid in the construction of a building—the one that finishes it off, the pièce de résistance. It's just as important as the first row, the foundation.

Since we spend more waking time at our workplace than at home, the place where we work is also, in effect, somewhere we live. The work we do there gives us the means to acquire the home we want, the "castle" where we feel we can relax; and it's generally true that the harder we work, the better we are able to afford a comfortable lifestyle at home. But imagine how much better your life would be if your workplace also promoted a happy, relaxed, stress-free state of mind!

If the environment where you spend eight or more waking hours each weekday is organized and managed well, if you are always prepared for whatever turns of events might occur, you will be more productive, more proactive, and ready to accept challenges. You will be ready to say, "Okay, world, give me your best shot." You'll be ready to perform, to turn negatives into positives. By eliminating the rushed feeling that results from disorganization, you'll have a clear mind. The power of positive thinking will be a thrust engine within you, ready to move forward with new ideas and concepts, ready to commit, willing to take risks that you were not ready to take before.

You know what you have to do to get your workspace organized. You know where the clutter is—or you'll soon find out. Follow the method you have already applied at home, and make it work. Finish the last space around you. You will be ready and rehearsed, trained for learning to manage your time.

Remember, though, the maintenance of the space around you must always be prioritized. If there is no follow-through, if clutter resurfaces, your opportunity to learn to manage your time will diminish and disappear. But you are not going to allow that to happen. You have already experienced the rewards of managing the space around you and the gift of extra time in your day. By continuing the process, you are becoming that accomplished, self-managed person you always wanted to be, cruising smoothly through life like a cyclist who has learned to pedal consistently to make it easily over the next hill. You will be in the best shape of your life, always prepared to win.

Ready to learn to manage your time? Absolutely!

STEP FOUR
of
SEVEN EASY STEPS

Learn to Manage Your Time in Your Own Environment, Without Changing Who You Are

Helper Items for managing your time can be found in the mail-order source section, Step Six, page 99.

1. **Appointment book.**
2. **PDA/Personal Digital Assistant.**
3. **Calendar.**
4. **Clocks.**
5. **Notepads.**

Time is where it all starts—past, present, and future. Time has been there from the beginning, throughout the duration of all existence.

When we awake each morning, we are given the gift of time all over again. It is what we do with each hour, how we manage it, that gives each day its meaning. That is also what gives meaning to life itself, since our lifetime is made up of as many days as we are given, one at a time. Learning to manage our time is learning how make the gift of life our number-one priority.

There is a beginning and an end to each hour, each day, each week, each month, each year, each lifetime. We are all making choices, all the time, about how we spend those hours, days, weeks and months, January through December. The ancient Romans named the first month of the year Janus for their "god of doorways and the rising and setting of the sun"—represented by one head with two faces looking in opposite directions. Ever since, January has been regarded as a time to reflect on the past and apply valuable lessons to the future, to look back at the previous year and forward to the year that is just beginning.

No matter which month or day it may be on the calendar as you are reading these words, consider it the first of January. And, when you

75

awake tomorrow morning, consider it another new beginning. It is! (As is the next day, and the next, and the one after that.) Your goal is to learn how to effectively manage the minutes and hours contained in each day. If you do, as days become weeks, months and years, you will have gained an amazing amount of extra time—two hours each day to spend with yourself, your family and friends.

My philosophy in learning how to manage my time was to take a good look at where it had been going and to redirect it to serve me better. I learned to incorporate my activities into a daily schedule that would work in my environment, according to my personality and preferences.

Successfully managing your time is an art, and to learn how to do it takes . . . well, time. Yes, that is the first step in Step Four. You must allocate time in your mind for this, commit to wanting to do it. Try bringing more awareness to how your subconscious mind interacts with your conscious mind, and enable the subconscious to more actively support you in your current goals.

A good place to begin is to do a little evaluation of your personal life and your work life. Determine whether any change is needed—and if it is, trust and accept that the change will do you good. Like Janus, reflect on the past and look toward the future. With the clarity of mind you've earned as a side benefit of the new, streamlined way you are now managing your home and workplace, you will be better pre-pared to welcome what comes next.

As you make appropriate changes in your life, you'll find that you are becoming more comfortable with yourself, more relaxed. Relaxation, in turn, promotes happiness. All are extensions of managing your time well—eliminating rush and stress. When you have learned to manage your time, you will be able to look at situations objectively and turn negatives into positives. You will be able to set attainable goals, and review them periodically to see whether they require modification.

One of the most important elements in managing your time effectively is to take advantage of your most productive hours in each day—the time of day when you are at your best. Many of us are at peak productivity in the morning hours. Others may feel a burst of energy, a second wind, in late evening. It is essential to know who you are, how you function. If some change seems to be needed, try it on to make sure it fits with your style, your personality.

It's also important to discover which activities (and "inactivities") must be included in your day to create a sense of balance. Beginning when you awake and continuing throughout the day, take notice when you feel balanced, centered . . . and when you don't. You may find that not doing a certain thing at a certain time of day—or forgoing it altogether—is at least as important to your quality of life as it is to *do* other things. When you are comfortable with yourself and your choices, each day will be a better, happier day.

Organizing your time is a parallel activity to organizing the space around you. You have learned to fit objects into the rooms of your house so that the items are accessible and the rooms are not crowded. In a similar way, fitting what you want to accomplish each day onto the blank piece of paper that will contain your daily task schedule will require prioritization.

Managing your time can become an art, one that lends beauty and grace to each day, but only if you are realistic. Practice asking yourself, "Do I really need to do that?" "Do I really want to spend time with that acquaintance?" Remember, each and every day, we all make choices about how we spend our gift of time. If we make our choices honestly and with self-knowledge, we will feel that we are using our day in ways that benefit us best.

Part of learning to manage your time is learning to say no. Not to spend that extra time on the telephone. To develop a routine and become consistent with it. If self-discipline has never been part of your daily life, perhaps this would be a good opportunity to see where it fits in. No need to worry: I'm not suggesting that you suddenly become a controlled, structured person. You are who you are, and we're not changing that. Discipline (or, if you prefer another word, commitment) can come in small doses.

If you are going to manage your time successfully, you must have an agreement with yourself—an agreement to follow through on what you commit yourself to do in your daily task schedule. You may be wondering, though, just when you're going to sleep if you commit and follow through on all of those self-assigned tasks that seem genuinely important. I understand. It really can seem that there just are not enough hours in the day.

If you tend to have an agenda packed with more than you can handle and often find yourself without the time or energy to complete the things you start, prioritizing must become your priority. At first it may seem that many or all of the tasks on your list are equally important and urgent. Once you have established a daily task routine, however, you will start to recognize what is actually most important to get done, and you'll begin to trust yourself to make the call.

You will become accomplished at the art of prioritizing as you begin to realize that some or many of the things you once believed *had* to be done were things that other people seem to find important, but—what do you know!—you can live just fine without. Your list will probably start to change as you begin to live "according to your own lights" instead of in someone else's shadow. (Just because your dad, your mother-in-law, your neighbor, or Martha Stewart does something doesn't mean *you* have to do it—even if it seems somewhat admirable.)

With practice, you will start to become comfortable with creating a realistic task list within your daily routine. Once you start to get the hang of prioritizing, you will begin to realize you have developed not just a skill, but a rhythm. You'll be finishing the most urgent tasks first, eliminating stress and pressure. With the big ones out of the way, the smaller daily tasks are no big deal.

Time Readiness

Organizing your time means being ready: being prompt and completely prepared for action, without hesitation. Being ready means that you are managing your time well, and you are always prepared to recognize, accept, and deal with opportunities. Having good time-management skills will save you at least two hours each day and enable you to handle just about anything that comes along—career opportunities, social events, personal and family decisions.

You won't be living like Jeanette, who wasted countless hours looking for her glasses. Jeanette didn't need glasses for reading—just basic seeing. To read, she would remove them—and would never remember where she had placed them. Once, after searching in every area of her home, she decided to look in the medicine cabinet, recalling that she had removed her glasses to read the back of a medication bottle. When she looked in the mirror, she found them . . . on top of her head. With no awareness of how much time she was losing, Jeanette had come to accept the glasses search as part of her lifestyle. She had no idea that she was spending at least a couple of hours a week wandering around the house, looking for a way to see clearly.

Then there was Barry, who lost at least a few hours every day to doubling back. A fine carpenter, one of the best, Barry worked by himself and lived by himself, but his daily task schedule never got completed—mainly because he didn't have one. The problem started again every morning, when Barry could be relied on to be late for his first appointment or his arrival on the job site. He would leave his home in the morning, walk out to his truck, and remember to remember what he'd forgotten. So, back to the house he would go, not just once, but two or three times. Occasionally he'd start the truck, or even drive a mile or two, before remembering one more thing. Barry blamed it on his age. He claimed that ever since turning 56, he couldn't remember anything—including his age.

Jeanette and Barry had two things in common—no schedule of daily tasks, and no awareness of the high cost of their habit of forgetfulness.

Assuming that you are in good health, forgetfulness is not usually a result of memory loss. It is a result of having no constructive routine, and no real understanding of what lost time means at the end of the day. Jeanette and Barry were never Time Ready. They had a routine, but the wrong routine. They'd become accustomed to working around their ingrained bad habits—as if they were humoring a cranky baby or an inflexible old uncle. Rather than trying to improve on how they managed their time, they just let it slip by. Once past, those hours were gone for good. Each day, these two well-meaning human beings were squandering the gift of time they'd been given when they opened their eyes that morning.

Time Awareness

Since managing your time is the sequel to managing the space around you, we're going to go back briefly to revisit the sequential method we used in getting your home organized.

Your day's gift of time begins in the bedroom, with the moments when you first wake up. The more efficient you can be at the very start of the day, the more productive your day will be. Yes, I know, some of us are not morning people, and may take a little more time to get going than others. We're all different, and that's okay. But whatever schedule your "biorhythms" are on, Time Awareness is important. It's no problem if it takes you a few hours in the morning to get rolling, get the blood flowing to all brain cells, as long as you are aware of time passing and you are consistently using it to your benefit.

Time Awareness converts into Time Readiness. By making these two qualities part of your daily routine, you will be taking a giant step forward. You will sit up and notice if hours, or even minutes, begin passing you by.

Managing your time effectively at home, where your day starts, will contribute to your productivity at work and to your sense of calm and pleasure as you spend time at leisure, with family, and with friends. Your days will become more fluid and fulfilling.

Leaving your home at a scheduled time in the morning, with no stress or rush, will give you an advantage throughout the day. You will arrive at work on time and be more relaxed and productive. The qualities you bring with you at your departure time will become your attitude, your style. Being Time Ready will become second nature, and you will be happier. It will be much easier to laugh with others, even if you're laughing at yourself. A Time Ready person has many special days.

Your Daily Task Schedule

There is a beginning to everything. Developing a daily task list, fitting everything you want to accomplish in a given day onto a blank sheet of paper, takes a little time—but it's time well invested. You're spending a little in order to save a lot. The more time you can save, the more good times you will have.

A task schedule is your road map through the day. If you try to find your way through new territory without a map, it's like going to the grocery store without a shopping list. What happens? It takes longer and you end up forgetting most of the items you need, which means you have to go back, which means you've lost time. And you've probably wasted time and money bringing home things you don't need.

How do you decide what to include on your schedule?

Begin by blocking out the hours that are non-negotiable—those that are already dedicated to your job and to such essential life-support activities as eating and sleeping, or childcare. Next, on a piece of scrap paper, list the tasks and activities you feel are important to accomplish on that particular day. At the side of each one, note a realistic approximation of the time it should take from start to finish. When you think the list is complete, add up the total time required, and compare it with the time you actually have available. If you've gone overboard, prioritize and add it up again. When the time required matches the time you have, fill in the slots on your actual schedule.

The best time to start formulating your thinking for the upcoming day's tasks is during the current day, during a break at work or while commuting. As part of being Time Ready, have notepaper accessible wherever you are for task notations. Making notes when thoughts occur is task prep. Your notes can be consolidated during the evening, and finalized the next morning. Remember, though, to cut yourself some slack. Although the best time to create your task list is the day and evening before, that won't always work in reality.

Nor will it always be possible to finish everything on the list, no matter how well you may have prioritized it. Having a balanced perspective includes getting to the point where you can say, without guilt, "I can't always get it all done in a day." You betcha. That's right. Part of flexibility is accepting that there will be days when it doesn't happen. Then, what next? You guessed it—a rewrite of the previous daily task list, incorporating it into the present day.

You may be thinking that I'm making a daily task list sound like a career, but all this will be second nature soon. Your schedule is your guide, your road map, to your daily goals. And it will save much more time than it takes—I promise!

With your task list completed and waiting for you when you awaken in the morning, your day will begin with direction. You are Time Ready, up and at it, with a schedule to guide you through the hours with Time Awareness. You are now aware of what you want to accomplish in this window of opportunity called time.

Other preparations you can do the previous day to help launch your morning with ease include organizing your clothing, especially if any ironing is required. If you have young children, decide on their clothing the prior evening as well. If they take lunch with them, prepare it before going to bed. Any other items you'll need in order to accomplish your daily tasks should be ready to go when you are ready to leave. Bills and letters to be mailed, clothing to be dropped at the cleaners—whatever is going out the door with you—should be prepared the evening before. If you are a coffee drinker, set up the automatic coffeemaker before you go to bed. If your car needs gas, tank it up during the day in order to be Time Ready in the morning. The more organized you are, the better the next day will flow.

Certainly, not everything will always go as planned. Glitches come with the territory, and they're sure to surface occasionally. But when you're organized, you're ready to deal with sudden surprises.

The thrust, the power, the energy that drives you is an outgrowth of your home environment. Your home is your support system, the key to keeping you Time Ready. You can now move through your morning with confidence and control, getting out the door with no stress and no mess. If you keep your home base of operation organized according to Step Three, you will become very successful at managing your time. If you get the hang of Putting It Back, your refuge will always be ready for your return at the end of the day. Your home will be an inviting place for you and your family, a soothing place to spend your time— the foundation of the relaxing lifestyle you deserve.

Between your home and your workplace, you have transportation time—most likely by car, train, or bus. Those minutes or hours belong to you: they are what you make them. Some people use their commute to regain tranquility—to think, meditate, rest, or read (assuming they're not behind the wheel). You might want to use this time to review and refine your daily task schedule, or get a jump on the next day's workload. The choice revolves around your personality, your style, and the idiosyncrasies of that particular day. Making good use of the present moment rewards you with future hours, which can be spent relaxing with family and friends.

Recent technological advances have given the world we live in a racecar momentum. The only way to feel at ease—to feel at the end of the day that it went the way you wanted it to go—is to be organized, able to manage the day's events and the time they consume. At this level, you are taking charge of your life and eliminating stress.

One of the learned skills in good time management is recognizing internal and external conditions, and consciously separating them when they surface in your day. An internal condition in your environment is one that has been brought on by you, so you can probably analyze it easily and determine how to deal with it. An external condition is an event that occurs outside of your control, and you may have to step back from it in order to see whether or not there is anything you can do about it. Having the ability to identify which things you can control (and which things you can't) comes with having a clear mind and the sense of calm that results from managing your time successfully.

With time and space management as your most essential tools, your mind will become a fine instrument, always prepared and ready to deal with sudden changes in internal or external conditions. You will be a balanced person with the ability to respond to any given situation with precise, clear decision-making.

TIME-MANAGEMENT GUIDELINES
and ORGANIZATION TIPS

We tend to perform many of the same tasks each day without noticing how long they take. Once you have mastered Time Awareness, however, you will be able to estimate how long any given task will take, and you'll have a handle on how to fit each of your daily activities into your schedule so that all runs smoothly.

In reclaiming those two extra hours, clocks are good tools. Yes, I know, you already have a few, but I'm suggesting taking it a step further. Your Time Awareness will increase if you have a clock in each room you pass through in your home. Sounds like overkill, you say? No, clocks are time-reference tools, and since time will be passing in each and every room, it can be of benefit to have easy access to a time-keeper wherever you may be. Time reference becomes Time Awareness, preparing you to be Time Ready. Think of the clocks as training aids.

Another simple, integral part of time management is always having a means at hand of jotting down notes. Notepads in whatever style works for you should be strategically placed throughout your home, your workplace, and your car. To avoid increasing the clutter factor, keep them accessible but out of the way—at the front of a drawer, or neatly arranged in a corner. Place them near each telephone, by your favorite easy chair, on your desk, on your bedside table, and, yes, in the bathroom and the kitchen. Put a small notepad in your pocket when you take a walk.

Thoughts pass through the mind in nanoseconds, and they can be difficult to track or hold onto beyond the fleeting moment when they occur. So many great thoughts have been lost for a lack of notepaper! Having accessible notepads gives you the ability to capture those thoughts, lasso them and pull them in. Good ideas can turn into great ideas—if you jot them down.

The Paper Chase

Wherever possible, downsize your bookkeeping process. Keep as many elements as simple as possible, and you will save time by being more efficient. I recommend the following:

Online banking—Provides instant action at your fingertips. You can easily view statements and current balance information, while eliminating paper records—saving trees and time.

Online brokerage statements—With just a click, you can see your account status. No waiting for monthly statements. Eliminates paper and saves time.

Mail sorting—Incoming mail should be sorted by category. Bills should be marked with arrival date and due date, and filed in the "unpaid" file. Establish a designated bill-paying day each week. You will always know where the bills are, and you'll never have to wonder whether they've been paid by the due date. More saved time.

Income tax folder—At the beginning of each year, establish a folder for filing mail and records pertaining to that year's taxes. The IRS has a website that recommends the length of time you should keep records from previous calendar years; or you can consult your accountant or an accounting service. Keeping a folder for current tax year information will save time during the income tax filing period.

Calendar, appointment book, PDA (Personal Digital Assistant)—Use whatever format works best for you, as long as you have some sort of efficient system to record important family dates, social events, birthdays and anniversaries, doctor appointments, and vacations. All of these dates should be entered as soon as you are aware of them. If you receive an invitation to a function that requires an RSVP, the date should be entered and the RSVP done at once, to save time and energy later. The calendar should be placed where it is visible and accessible. Appointment books and PDAs are generally portable, so you'll be carrying yours along with you and entering dates throughout the day; but when you arrive back home, keep it where you'll be able access it quickly if you need to make an entry.

Vehicle maintenance—This can seem to be a time-consuming task, but your car is your assistant. It must be reliable and healthy to be of service to you and to avoid such wastages of time and energy as breakdowns and flat tires. The down time associated with car maintenance can be productive time, too.

One Touch, One Time

Managing your time and the space around you is based on simplicity. One very basic and fundamental truth that applies across the board is: The fewer times you touch an object, the more time is saved. Your goal is "One Touch, One Time." And that is possible only if you Put It Back. If it's where it belongs, you won't be shifting it from place to place as you search for something else, or as you try to use the space it is wrongfully occupying.

Remember these phrases: One Touch, One Time; Time Awareness; and Time Ready. Making all three part of your mindset will allow you to progress quickly.

I have a friend who, when asked the question, "How are you doing?" consistently answers, "Superior." When you are asked, "How are you doing with managing your time and the space around you?" I want you to be able to answer, "Superior." If you are committed and consistent in following the Seven Steps, there will be no stopping you.

IF YOU FEEL TIME IS PASSING YOU BY, TAKE ANOTHER LOOK AT IT AS IT IS PASSING.

You will see pockets of opportunity opening.

Take advantage of those opportunities. Live life your way, as I am living it my way. You'll soon find your balance, your song, your rhythm.

STEP FIVE
of
SEVEN EASY STEPS

Acquiring the Tools to Organize the Space Around You

MAIL-ORDER SOURCES

In this section you'll find Helper Items that are recommended based on their functional application in organizing and managing the space around you (Step Three). Selections were made by reviewing several mail-order catalog companies that carry items designed to make household and workplace organization easier and more efficient. Helper Items that made the cut represent the best value and quality available. Many of them I have used personally; others are recommended solely on their appearance and description in the catalog. The catalog's reputation for quality products and reliable customer service has also been taken into consideration.

Some of these items may appear to be pricey at first glance, but their cost accurately reflects their value, quality, and functional use. Availability and price were confirmed prior to the printing of this book, but they are, of course, subject to change. Since you'd probably prefer to have a visual picture of an item prior to making your purchase, you might want to call the company to request a catalog, or go online to their website to save time and avoid creating clutter. Check your catalog pile first, though. You may just find what you're looking for.

While Helper Items are essential to your success, I want you to be practical about this approach. Before dialing an 800 number or clicking online to purchase a product, check your closets, cabinets, drawers, garage, attic, and basement to see whether you already have some of these items. If you do, or even if you find some things that are similar in function, kudos! You have just saved money and time. Make a list of the items you have on hand and stash them in a convenient location where you can find them easily when you're ready to start.

Once you're ready to begin, approach the process methodically in order to avoid overload, stress, and new clutter. Go through your home and determine the spaces you think you could reorganize in one segment. Assess how long the process will take. For example, make a realistic assessment of the time you think it will take to reorganize your bedroom, bathroom, and bedroom closet. Ask yourself whether you think you'll be able to reorganize these areas in one weekend and, perhaps, some evenings, or whether taking on all three spaces at once will mean overload. Decide realistically what will work best for you.

Having the right Helper Items will prevent new clutter buildup while removing old clutter, and establishing a fairly accurate time estimate will help avoid the buildup of new stress.

HELPER ITEMS
Bedroom

Cedar drawer dividers—Home Trends catalog, www.hometrendscatalog.com, 1-800-810-2340. Item #201046, 13" x 12¾" x 3¾", $9.95 each.

Her jewelry box—Hammacher Schlemmer catalog, www.hammacherschlemmer.com, 1-800-321-1484. Item #61867, $79.95.

His watch/money valet—Lizell, www.lizell.com, 1-800-718-8882. Item #12K238, $49.95. Black, tan, mahogany.

Brinks safe—Frontgate, www.frontgate.com, 1-800-626-6488. Item #1795, 11⅞" W x 5" H x 14" D, 18 lbs, $119.95.

Bathroom

Space-saver cabinet for over the toilet—Home Decorators Collection, www.homedecorators.com, 1-800-245-2217. Item #20657, 68½" H x 27" W x 10½" D, black or white, $169.00.

Cedar drawer dividers—Home Trends catalog, www.hometrendscatalog.com, 1-800-810-2340. Item #201046, 13" x 12¾" x 3¾", $9.95 each.

Cedar dividers for deep drawers—Always Organized catalog, www.alwaysorganized.com, 1-800-849-7210. Item #HEL 6115, 12"W x 4"H x 12"D, $9.95.

Under-cabinet slide-out organizer—Sporty's catalog, www.sportys.com, 1-800-776-7897. Item #2987T, 11½"W x 11"D x 11"H, $24.95.

Under-cabinet slide-out trash pail—Improvements catalog, www.improvements.com, 1-800-642-2112. Item # 124867, 11" W x 16" D x 11"H, $24.99.

Floor waste bin—holdeverything catalog, www.holdeverything.com, 1-800-421-2264. Item #39-4510699, 8" SQ x 10½" H, $44.00.

Toilet bowl brush—holdeverything catalog, www.holdeverything.com, 1-800-421-2264. Item #39-4016044, 17" H x 3½"D, $29.00. Stainless steel.

Soap dish/lotion dispenser/toothbrush holder—holdeverything catalog, www.holdeverything.com, 1-800-421-2264. Item #45-00252, $44.00.

Facial tissue dispenser—holdeverything catalog, www.holdeverything.com, 1-800-421-2264. Item #39-4510699, $24.00.

Towel bar—holdeverything catalog, www.holdeverything.com, 1-800-421-2264. Item #39-4015897, 18" x 3" x 2½", $34.00; 24" x 3" x 2½", $39.00. Porcelain/chrome finish.

Towel hooks—holdeverything catalog, www.holdeverything.com, 1-800-421-2264. Item #39-4015897, 2½" x 3¼" x 2½", 2 for $29.00.

Towel rings—Pottery Barn catalog, www.potterybarn.com, 1-800-922-5507. Item #41-69926, 6½" D, $29.00.

Closet

Cedar wardrobe closet—Home Trends catalog, www.hometrendscatalog.com, 1-800-810-2340. Item #039134, 35.1"W x 19"D x 61"H, $69.95. Locate where space is available, in attic or basement.

Jumbo clear storage bag—Home Trends catalog, www.hometrends.catalog.com, 1-800-810-2340. Item #034058, $10.95. Locate where space is available.

Shelf dividers—Home Trends catalog, www.hometrendscatalog.com, 1-800-810-2340. Item #005604, 4.8" H x 9"D, $14.95.

Plastic hangers—Home Trends catalog, www.hometrendscatalog.com, 1-800-810-2340. Item #016620, set of 36 "Champ" hangers, $21.95.

Tie/belt organizer—Sporty's catalog, www.sportys.com, 1-800-776-7897. Item #2758T, $29.00.

Multiple pant/trouser hanger—Hammacher Schlemmer catalog, www.hammacherschlemmer.com, 1-800-321-1484. Item #61588, 20"H x 17"W, holds 10, $39.95. Item #61587, 40"H x 17"W, holds 20, $59.95.

Spring-tension rod—Vita Futura Company, www.vitafutura.com. Extends from 29.5" to 49.2", $22.99; or extends from 49.2 to 86.6", $28.99. White or aluminum. Recommended for blouses and light shirts only. Available online, or at your local hardware store.

Hanging baseball cap holder—Sporty's catalog, www.sportys.com, 1-800-776-7897. Item #1591T, $21.95. Holds up to 40 caps.

Wall hat rack—Home Decorators catalog, www.homedecorators.com, 1-800-245-2217. Item #24437, $29.00. A multi use, three-hook rack for hats and coats.

Door shoe rack—Improvements catalog, www.improvementscatalog.com, 1-800-642-2112. Item #168096, 22"W x 8"D x 78"H, $39.99. Holds up to 36 pairs.

Vinyl shoe storage hanging bag—Home Trends catalog, www.hometrendscatalog.com, 1-800-810-2340. Item #D036077, $12.95. Holds up to 9 pairs.

Under-bed rolling shoe storage—Improvements catalog, www.improvementscatalog.com, 1-800-642-2112. Item #154158, 39"W x 21"D x 2½"H, $16.99.

Under-bed drawer—Sporty's Preferred Living catalog, www.sportys.com, 1-800-776-7897. Item #102461, 24.1"D x 24"W x 6"H, $79.00. Cedar storage case.

Brinks safe—Frontgate catalog, www.frontgate.com, 1-800-626-6488. Item #1795, 11⅞"W x 5"H x 14"D, 18 lbs, $119.00. Use in dresser drawer or on closet shelf.

Mini Stepladder—Improvements catalog, www.improvementscatalog.com, 1-800-642-2112. Item #111344, $39.99.

Kitchen

Trash pullout slider—Improvements catalog, www.improvementscatalog.com, 1-800-642-2112. Item #124878, 14"W x 15½"D x 20"H, $29.99.

Under-sink slide-out shelf—Improvements catalog, www.improvementscatalog.com, 1-800-642-2112. Item #152859, 11⅛"W x 22"D x 2"H, $19.99.

Spice drawer organizer—holdeverything catalog, www.holdeverything.com, 1-800-421-2264. Item #39-4351508, 6½"W x 17"D x 1½"H, $19.00.

Condiment Lazy Susan rack—holdeverything catalog, www.holdeverything.com, 1-800-421-2264. Item #394486403, 11"D x 8"H, $39.00.

Cutlery organizer—Sporty's Preferred Living catalog, www.sportys.com, 1-800-359-7794. Item# 5000L, 11¼"W x 13¾" L x 2¼"D, $39.95.

Kitchen knife holder—Organize Everything Company, www.organize-everything.com, 1-800-600-9817. Item #357lI, 9⅛"W x 16¾"D x 2"H, $57.00. Fits in kitchen drawer.

Junk drawer organizer—Home Trends catalog, www.hometrendscatalog.com, 1-800-810-2340. Item #201190, $9.95.

Fridge can holder/dispenser—holdeverything catalog, www.holdeverything.com, 1-800-421-2264. Item #39-4355137, 18"D x 11"H x 5½" W, $34.00. Top holds additional items.

Butter dish—Kitchen Etc, www.kitchenetc.com, 1-800-663-8810. Item #SKU680397, $7.00. Acrylic. Recommended only if your fridge does not already contain one. It would be less expensive to purchase one locally.

Egg tray—Improvements catalog, www.improvementscatalog.com, 1-800-642-2112. Item #220753, $5.99. Recommended only if your fridge does not already contain one. Less expensive to purchase locally.

Pantry door organizer—Improvements catalog, www.improvementscatalog.com, 1-800-642-2112. Item #220428, 18"W x 72"H, $29.99. Item #220479, 24"W x 72"H, $39.99. Eight shelves.

Pantry tiered slide-out storage basket—Improvements catalog, www.improvementscatalog.com, 1-800-642-2112. Item #189311, 13"H x 8½"W x 18"D, $12.99.

Folding hideaway stool—Improvements catalog, www.improvementscatalog.com, 1-800-642-2112. Item #218669, 9" H, folds down to 2"W for easy storage, $14.99.

Hanging cookware rack—Improvements catalog, www.improvementscatalog.com, 1-800-642-2112. Item #225726, 32½"L x 17"W, $44.99. Can hang down as low as 22" from the ceiling, 20 hooks.

Baking tray cabinet dividers—Ovis On Line, www.ovisonline.com, 1-800-326-6847. Item # 597-12CR-52, 18" divider, $9.40. Item #597-18CR-52, 20" divider, $10.45.

Cookbook caddy—holdeverything catalog, www.holdeverything.com, 1-800-421-2264. Item #39-4482139 (Harvest basket), 8"x 5" 10", $24.00. Basket not designated as a caddy in catalog.

Pot lid under-cabinet pullout organizer—Sporty's catalog, www.sportys.com, 1-800-776-7897. Item #1656T, 22.1"D x 3¼"W x 3"H, $15.95.

Instant breakfast bar and stools—Alsto's catalog, www.alsto.com, 1-800-447-0048. Item #F87232-00D, 33"H x 28"H x 29½"D, $129.95.

Mail center/key rack—Improvements catalog, www.improvementscatalog.com, 1-800-642-2112. Item #160922, 10¾"H x 10¾"W x 3⅛"D, $24.95. Combination mail center and key storage. Place near main entry/exit door. (Also listed in backdoor/mudroom area.)

Living Room

Magazine rack—Crate and Barrel catalog, www.crateandbarrel.com, 1-800-323-5461. Item #24004, 11"W x 16½"L x 15"H, $39.95.

Remote control caddy—Sporty's catalog, www.sportys.com, 1-800-776-7897. Item #4359l, $39.00.

Wall-hanging bookshelf—Home Decorators catalog, www.homedecorators.com, 1-800-245-2217. Item #16233, 32"H x 36"W x 6"D, $129.00. White, black, natural, dark cherry.

Floor-standing bookcase—Crate and Barrel catalog, www.crateandbarrel.com, 1-800-323-5461. Item #74010, 25½" x 14" x 76"H, $159.00.

Wall-hanging framed photo shelf—Home Decorators catalog, www.homedecorators.com, 1-800-245-2217. Item #02007, 18"H x 18"W x 4"D, $44.00. Light walnut, white, black, natural, dark cherry.

CD drawer organizer—Staples catalog, www.staples.com, 1-800-378-2753. Item #384339, $10.73. Holds up to 40 CDs; can be stored in a drawer.

Floor-standing CD tower—Home Decorators catalog, www.homedecorators.com, 1-800-245-2217. Item #25311, 48½"H x 13½"W x 7"D, $89.00. Cherry, black, oak.

Photo frames—Pottery Barn catalog, www.potterybarn.com, 1-800-922-5507. Item #66-2001667, 4x6 single, $20.00; 4x6 double, $25.00; 4x6 triple, $29.00; 8x10 grouping of nine 4x6's, $55.00. Black, white, mahogany with matting.

Coffee-table book tiered bookstand—Pottery Barn catalog, www.potterybarn.com, 1-800-922-5507. Item #66-4337515, 18" x 16" x 53"H, $119.00. Antique white, distressed black.

End table storage—Home Decorators catalog, www.homedecorators.com, 1-800-245-2217. Item #12527, 32"H x 21½"W x 14½"D, $159.00. Light oak, honey, light cherry, chestnut.

Storage ottoman—Home Decorators catalog, www.homedecorators.com, 1-800-245-2217. Item #21459, 14" H x 24"W x 15"D, $80.00. Hunter green, burgundy, ivory.

Home Bill Paying/Office/Desk/Communications

Two-drawer file cabinet—Home Decorators catalog, www.homedecorators.com, 1-800-245-2217. Item #13600, 29"H, $119.00. Wood, mahogany, white, washed oak. Or Staples, www.staples.com, 1-800-378-2753. Item #489530, 28¼" H, $89.99. Metal, tan, black.

Small accordion-pocket folder—Staples, www.staples.com, 1-800-378-2753. Item #874893, $11.88. Twelve expandable pockets.

Large accordion-pocket folder—Staples, www.staples.com, 1-800-378-2753. Item #493209, expands up to 31 pockets, $29.99

Portable file—Staples, www.staples.com, 1-800-378-2753. Item #432252, 11⅛"H x 13"L x 3"W x 10¾"D, $12.59.

Hanging file folders—Staples, www.staples.com, 1-800-378-2753. Item #266262, 50 for $7.99.

Regular file folders—Staples, www.staples.com, 1-800-378-2753. Item #45829, 50 for $10.45.

File labels—Staples, www.staples.com, 1-800-378-2753. Item #165787, 248 for $1.99.

Metropolitan cork bulletin board —Pottery Barn catalog, www.potterybarn.com, 1-800-922-5507. Item #66-3676848, 21" x 24", $99.00.

Portable desktop holder—Staples, www.staples.com, 1-800-378-2753. Item #202192, $15.74. Holds pens, pencils, rubber bands, paperclips.

Notepads—Staples, www.staples.com, 1-800-378-2753. Item #534180, 12 pads for $8.79.

Wall "At a Glance" Calendar—Staples, www.staples.com, 1-800-378-2753. Item #2004, $11.99.

Weekly-monthly planner/address book—Staples, www.staples.com, 1-800-378-2753. Item # 481089, $23.99.

Personal Digital Assistant/PDA—Staples, www.staples.com, 1-800-378-2753. Item #480200, $174.99.

Letter opener—Staples, www.staples.com, 1-800-378-2753. Item #458232, $1.27.

Pencils—Staples, www.staples.com, 1-800-378-2753. Item #327694, 24 for $10.79.

Pens—Staples, www.staples.com, 1-800-378-2753. Item #104703, 12 for $5.25.

Paperclips—Staples, www.staples.com, 1-800-378-2753. Item #472480, 1 box, $1.48.

Rubber Bands—Staples, www.staples.com, 1-800-378-2753. Item #36311, pack of assorted sizes, $2.49.

Swingline stapler—Staples, www.staples.com, 1-800-378-2753. Item#272120, $4.59 with staples.

Ruler—Staples, www.staples.com, 1-800-378-2753. Item #505982, $0.32.

Tape—Staples, www.staples.com, 1-800-378-2753. Item #483534, 4 rolls with dispenser, $3.07.

Blank and letterhead envelopes—Purchase locally.

Scissors—Staples, www.staples.com, 1-800-378-2753. Item #711770, $3.79.

Desk-drawer tray—Staples, www.staples.com, 1-800-378-2753. Item #37882, 14"W x 9"D x 1⅛"H, $3.49.

Calculator—Staples, www.staples.com, 1-800-378-2753. Item #44091, Canon LS 82Z, hand held, $9.95

Laundry Room

Ironing center—Sporty's catalog, www.sportys.com, 1-800-776-7897.
Item #2644T, iron holder, 13"H x 7"W x 4"D;
board holder 5"H x 5½"W x 2½"D, $13.75. Ironing board not included.

Tension clothes hanger—Improvements catalog,
www.improvementscatalog.com, 1-800-642-2112. Item #191919, $29.99.
Ceiling to floor, instant installation with 7' to 10.5' ceiling height.

Hanging wall shelf—Sporty's catalog, www.sportys.com, 1-800-776-7897.
Item #1948T, $12.50.

Ironing board cabinet—Improvements catalog,
www.improvementscatalog.com, 1-800-642-2112. Item #169259,
47⅞"H x 15"W x 3"D, $199.95.

Lint trash pail—Crate and Barrel catalog, www.crateandbarrel.com,
1-800-323-5464. Item #64077, 15"H, $8.95.

Powder Room

Counter hand-towel rack—Home Decorators catalog,
www.homedecorators.com, 1-800-245-2217. Item #20641, 12½"H, $19.00.

Facial tissue dispenser—holdeverything catalog, www.holdeverything.com,
1-800-421-2264. Item #39-4565206, $14.00.

Bucket candles – Crate and Barrel catalog, www.crateandbarrel.com,
1-800-323-5461. Item #94003, $12.95.

Soap dish—holdeverything catalog, www.holdeverything.com,
1-800-421-2264. Item #39-4500252, $14.00.

Trash pail/waste bin—holdeverything catalog, www.holdeverything.com,
1-800-421-2264. Item #39-4510699, 8"SQ x 10½"H, $44.00.

Front-Entry and Backdoor Closets

Plastic hangers—Home Trends catalog, www.hometrendscatalog.com,
1-800-810-2340. Item #016620, 36 heavy-duty "Champ" hangers, $21.95.

Wood hangers—holdeverything catalog, www.holdeverything.com,
1-800-421-2264. Item #39-4015624, set of six, $29.00.

Duster and broom—Improvements catalog, www.improvementscatalog.com, 1-800-642-2112. Duster, item #196825, $17.95. Broom, item #216412, $19.95.

Dustpan—Sporty's catalog, www.sportys.com, 1-800-776-7897. Item #2008T, $8.95.

Dust buster—Tyler Tool Company, www.store.yahoo.com, 1-800-222-8401. Item #V4810, $29.95.

Wall Tool Bracket—Improvements catalog, www.improvementscatalog.com, 1-800-642-2112. Item #210076, 10½" W, $13.99.

Wall-hanging hat rack—Home Decorators catalog, www.homedecorators.com, 1-800-245-2217. Item #24437, $29.00. Multi-purpose three-hook hat and coat rack.

Attic and Basement

Cedar wardrobe closet—Home Trends catalog, www.hometrendscatalog.com, 1-800-810-2340. Item #039134, 35.1"W x 19"D x 61"H, $69.95. Jumbo storage bag, item #034058, $10.95.

Open plastic shelving—Sporty's catalog, www.sportys.com, 1-800-776-7897. Item #9885T, $45.95.

Clear plastic storage boxes/drawers—holdeverything catalog, www.holdeverything.com, 1-800-421-2264. Item #4015657, 6¾" x 12½" x 4½", set of six, $49.00.

Garage

Pet food dispenser—Improvements catalog, www.improvementscatalog.com, 1-800-642-2112. Item #138107, $29.99.

Bike hoist/pulley system—Improvements catalog, www.improvementscatalog.com, 1-800-642-2112. Item #164655, $39.99. System attaches to ceilings up to 14'H.

Wall-hanging sports equipment storage—Sporty's catalog, www.sportys.com, 1-800-776-7897. Item #10078T, 52¾"W x 24½"H x 11½"D, $29.75. Holds baseballs, bats, and mitts; soccer balls; footballs; golf balls, tennis balls and racquets.

Five-station tool holder—Improvements catalog, www.improvementscatalog.com, 1-800-642-2112. Item #210776, $13.99. Hangs on wall.

Ceiling-mounted storage racks—Sporty's catalog, www.sportys.com, 1-800-776-7897. Item #1310T (large), $135.00; 21267T (small), $99.95.

Five-step safety ladder—Frontgate catalog, www.frontgate.com, 1-800-626-6488. Item #3016, 10½ lbs, $129.00.

Recycling bins—Plow and Hearth catalog, www.plowhearth.com, 1-800-494-7544. Item #4341, set of three, $49.95.

Roving garden caddy—Power House catalog, www.powerhousecatalog.com, 1-877-1777. Item #A604, $69.95. Stores tools, plants, and fertilizer.

Car/Trunk

Coat/jacket hanger—Power House catalog, www.powerhousecatalog.com, 1-877-1777. Item #A732, $24.95.

Lap desk—Auto Sport catalog, www.autosportcatalog.com, 1-800-726-1199. Item #1081, $39.00. Business Center multiple-pocket office with detachable lap desk.

Seat back organizer—Sporty's catalog, www.sportys.com, 1-800-776-7897. Item #1202T, $14.75.

Trash container—Sporty's catalog, www.sportys.com, 1-800-776-7897. Item #2128T, $12.95.

Clothes-hanging bar—Sporty's catalog, www.sportys.com, 1-800-776-7897. Item #1421T, $14.50.

Instant cargo trunk organizer—Auto Sport catalog, www.autosport.com, 1-800-726-1199. Item #84401, $79.95.

Glove-compartment assistant—Auto Sport catalog, www.autosport.com, 1-800-726-1199. Item #4030, $39.95. Designed to hold glove-compartment items; fastens on back of sun visor.

Backdoor/Mudroom

Jacket/coat rack—Home Decorators catalog, www.homedecorators.com, 1-800-245-2217. Item #24566, 17"W, $29.00. Six-hook rack.

Tiered cedar sports-shoe rack—Improvements catalog, www.improvementscatalog.com, 1-800-642-2112. Item #18139, 29½L x 12"H, $29.99.

Umbrella stand—Home Decorators catalog, www.homedecorators.com, 1-800-245-2217. Item #20161, 14"H, $39.00. Forest green.

Doormat—Home Decorators catalog, www.homedecorators.com, 1-800-245-2217. Item #22150 (Bengal), 2' x 3.5', $19.00.

Mail center/key rack—Improvements catalog, www.improvementscatalog.com, 1-800-642-2112. Item #160922, $24.95.

Trash Pails

An entire page in the Home Decorators catalog is devoted to **trash pails, waste bins, and wastebaskets**: www.homedecorators.com, 1-800-245-2217.

Purse/Shoulder Bag/Wallet/Money Clip/Briefcase

Purse—Coach catalog, www.coach.com, 1-888-262-6224. Item #6332, 22½" adjustable strap, 9"L x 5⅝"H x 4⅝" W, $158.00. Fabric with leather trim. Coach has a wide selection.

Women's shoulder bag—Travel Tools catalog, www.traveltools.com, 1-800-586-5676. Item #871, $69.95. Or Lizell catalog, www.lizell.com, 1-800-718-8882. Item #15K116, $129.00.

Women's wallet—Travel Tools catalog, www.traveltools.com, 1-800-586-5676. Item #A41, $59.95.

Men's money clip—Sharper Image catalog, www.sharperimage.com, 1-800-344-4494. Item #KT135, $34.95. Or Travel Tools catalog, www.traveltools.com, 1-800-586-5676. Item #Z01, $39.95.

Men's briefcase—Travel Tools catalog, www.traveltools.com, 1-800-586-5676. Item #B60, $129.95. Or Staples, www.staples.com, 1-800-378-2753. Item #440988, $59.99.

Men's wallet—Travel Tools catalog, www.traveltools.com, 1-800-586-5676. Item #A23, $30.95.

The application of Helper Items is just plain common sense: making good use of organizational tools. My goal is to encourage you to become successful at managing your space and your time, using some or all of these products. Once you start the process, you will probably discover other things that work well for you.

STEP SIX
of
SEVEN EASY STEPS

Acquiring the Tools for Managing Your Time

As we learned in Step Four, the essence of managing your time is simply being organized. Being organized keeps you Time Ready, with a clear mind that is capable of Time Awareness. There are few tools needed for this basic, fundamental process. Many of the required Helper Items were covered in Step Five, under Home Bill Paying/Office/Desk/Communications.

Weekly-monthly planner/address book/appointment book—Staples, www.staples.com, 1-800-378-2753. Item #481089, $23.99.

Personal Digital Assistant/PDA—Staples, www.staples.com, 1-800-378-2753. Item #480200, $174.99.

Wall "At a Glance" calendar—Staples, www.staples.com, 1-800-378-2753. Item #2004, $11.99.

Clocks—Staples, www.staples.com, 1-800-378-2753. Item #235853, 10" round wall clock, $14.29. Or item #439129, 13½" "Seth Thomas" Round Wall Clock, $18.75.

Or check out www.2timecontraptions.com, which offers clocks for every room in a variety of sizes, colors and prices.

Notepads—Staples, www.staples.com, 1-800-378-2753. Item #534180, 12 pads for $8.79.

STEP SEVEN
of
SEVEN EASY STEPS

**Your Daily Guide, or Tick System. An Outline Designed to
Assist You in Managing Your Time and the Space Around
You from Day to Day**

1. Awaken each day with a smile.

2. No clutter. Leave nothing out from the previous day or evening.
   Put It Back—One Touch, One Time.

3. Your home is your companion. It is a reflection of you, and sets
   the tone for your day. Keeping the space around you organized and
   managed will help you start each day with stability and a burst
   of energy.

4. You gotta have fun.

5. Remind yourself, "Time is our richest resource. It is what I do with
   it that is important." The choice is yours, so make the right choice.

6. Each evening, ask yourself, "What have I done with my time today?"

7. As the days, weeks, and months go by, ask yourself, "Have I been
   taking advantage of those pockets of opportunity?"

8. Continue to be aware of anything that has prevented you from
   being a better manager of your time and the space around you, and
   don't allow old habits to regain any ground.

9. A clear mind thrives in a clutter-free environment. If you find
   clutter creeping back into any area of your home or workplace,
   make a neat sign reading, CLEAR THE CLUTTER, CLEAR THE
   MIND. Place it where you will see it the next time you're tempted
   to let something slide into a pile.

10. Never allow pressure to build to up. Allow yourself to find your
    own rhythm each day as you manage your time and the space
    around you.

11. Get into the routine of a daily task schedule. Be flexible with it.

12. Allow your subconscious mind to work for you, cheering you on.

13. Always be aware of the value of your time. Notice if it's being wasted, and move on.

14. Remember, to be successful at managing your time, you must keep the space around you organized.

15. Remember, you can do it.

Thank you for reading *It's Your Time*. It has brought me great pleasure to share my thoughts with you in this book. I hope you can make the Seven Steps your own, and apply them in ways that will make your life more fulfilling.

Enjoy those extra two hours a day!

Ciao,

Joe Cirillo